# Jayne Mansfield
## and the
## American
## Fifties

MARTHA SAXTON

# Jayne Mansfield
## and the
## American
## Fifties

♥

Illustrated with photographs

Houghton Mifflin Company Boston

*1975*

Library of Congress Cataloging in Publication Data

Saxton, Martha.
Jayne Mansfield and the American Fifties

1. Mansfield, Jayne. I. Title.
PN2287.M37Sz   791.43'023'0924 [B]    74-28209
ISBN 0-395-20289-2

Printed in the United States of America

V 10 9 8 7 6 5 4 3 2 1

The poem on page 116 is reprinted with the permission of the
Macmillan Company from *The Collected Poems of W. B. Yeats*
by W. B. Yeats. Copyright © 1928 by the Macmillan Publish-
ing Company. Renewed 1956 by Georgie Yeats. Reprinted
by permission of M. B. Yeats, Miss Anne Yeats, Macmillan of
London & Basing-stoke and Macmillan.
The poem on page 198 is reprinted with the kind permission
of Karen Lindsey.

*To*

Josephine Stocking Saxton
*1912–1967*

# *Acknowledgments*

I am indebted to Muriel and Bill Davidson who put me up and put up with me during the California research. My thanks as well to Vera and Harry Peers, Charles Herschberg and Grace and Bill Shiffrin for their help. I would also like to thank Don Gold and Rob Cowley for their encouragement and interest.

# Contents

○ ○ ○ ○ ○ ○ ○ ○ ○ ○ ○ ○ ○ ○ ○ ○ ○ ○ ○ ○ ○ ○ ○ ○ ○ ○ ○ ○ ○ ○ ○ ○ ○ ○ ○

# *Illustrations*

*following page 104*

The essential Jayne Mansfield, in one of eleven bathrooms at the
   pink palace
Three-year-old Jayne in Phillipsburg
Jayne and Vera Peers, Dallas, 1946
Harry and Vera Peers with Paul Mansfield, Dallas, 1951
Jayne and matching Jayne Marie, Beverly Hills, 1954
Jayne and Tony Randall in subtle pas de deux in *Will Success Spoil
   Rock Hunter?*
Jayne at the champagne hour
Jayne's early love of animals never faltered
Jayne and Harry Peers before her marriage to Mickey at Portuguese
   Bend, California
Jayne and Mickey at the Peerses' wedding reception in Dallas
Jayne and Mickey arrive in Paris, 1959
The arms belong to Mickey
An American family
Mickey, Mickey, Jr., Jayne and Jayne Marie in front of Mickey's
   homemade avalanche at the pink palace
Vera at the piano in the pink palace, with Jayne Marie, Jayne and
   the Mickeys
Mickey observing Jayne's bra after her dress fell off in a Roman
   nightclub

o o o o o o o o o o o o o o o o o o o o o o o o o o o o o o o o o o o o o

# *Period Piece*

WOMEN'S HISTORY, unlike men's, is also the history of sex. If a woman transcends her sexual identity, it is with difficulty and cause for endless comment. If she doesn't, no one is surprised. A woman who capitalizes on it, on the other hand, is used or ridiculed. Feminists who have written about women naturally tend to gravitate toward heroines like Emma Goldman, Elizabeth Cady Stanton, Virginia Woolf and others who have struggled not to be seated in the back of the bus, who have fought to overcome the handicaps of their sex. It seemed to me equally important to examine the life of a woman who took her assigned role, exaggerated it, exploited it and played it out to its fatal conclusion. To understand what it means to be an exclusively sexual being, to understand why a woman chooses that part and what it does to her, will be a step toward understanding sex and its capacity to imprison or to free. Jayne Mansfield seemed like an obvious choice since she wasn't, on quick inspection, complex. Her career was sex and publicity, uncomplicated, I thought, by extraordinary talent or neurosis.

Jayne was the ur-sex object. She cultivated a walk which

○ ○ ○ ○ ○ ○ ○ ○ ○ ○ ○ ○ ○ ○ ○ ○ ○ ○ ○ ○ ○ ○ ○ ○ ○ ○ ○ ○ ○ ○ ○ ○ ○ ○ ○ ○ ○ ○ ○ ○

propelled her as far to the sides as it did forward. She mastered a high child's voice and a number of squeals and coos designed to prevent anyone from thinking her literate. In the fifties, Jayne was a demonstration of what to do and how to do it, when female sexuality was a come-on, a taste, a broken promise. Take a good look, she said, but don't touch. She taught lessons in artifice, enticement and hypocrisy. She sacrificed the fullness of her potential to what became a kind of isolated, burning narcissism which made her suspicious of men and cut her off from normal human contact, narrowing her range of feelings and vision. In her lopsidedness she came to believe that her only quality was her bust, and rather than fight for the rest of her, she lowered her spaghetti straps, giving herself over to the definition others gave her. There is no way to determine the cost of sacrificing infinite human possibilities to one physical fact.

She was a complicated event, Jayne. Only the fifties could have produced her. Like most women, she wasn't allowed to lead, but for a moment, she was a uniquely gifted and canny follower. She availed herself of the 1950s stereotypes about women, gathered them up and packaged them into the helpless, breathless, pouty tease which described sexy American women. She became an object lesson in the sex life of the fifties. If anyone characterized the schizoid attitude toward sex in this country, it was Jayne. She said piously that people paid too much attention to sex as she peeled off her bra and frolicked in bubble baths for photographers. She claimed to want to be a serious actress and went on stage in cellophane. In print she admired men for their spiritual qualities while in the flesh she married Mr. Universe. She presented her body to the nation for its sexual fantasies, talking all the while about her daughter's Brownie troop.

Jayne's talents don't explain the immense coverage she got. She wasn't a real beauty. Her singing was unexceptional and her violin playing on a par with Jack Benny's. Her acting was, at its best, enthusiastic. She was, however, shrewd, colossally stacked and insatiable for attention.

From one feminist point of view, Jayne was a classic woman-victim. She degraded herself, disguised her brains and relied for her identity on her ability to arouse sexual interest. On the other hand, there are many ways, within the dictates of a sex-obsessed culture, in which Jayne was liberated. If liberation includes making one's career as important as one's private life, mobilizing one's energies toward some goal distinct from being a wife and mother, then Jayne was at least partly free. She had fanatical determination in a period and in a country where fanatical determination isn't high on the list of womanly virtues. Had society not put such a premium on women with gargantuan bosoms and tiny little minds, the phenomenon of Jayne wouldn't have happened. On the other hand, it's hard to imagine circumstances under which Jayne would have chosen to be a civil engineer or a brain surgeon. One can make the case that she was exploited by a sexist culture. One can also make the not mutually exclusive case that she exploited that culture for all she and it were worth.

If Jayne was a product of the fifties, then she was a casualty of the sixties. In the fifties, Jayne and American men had conspired to keep sex a secret. By the sixties the secret was out. The pill and the sexual revolution on the campuses had begun eating away at the double standard. Women who had come on now followed through. It was no longer a choice between marrying and burning. No one had to do either. This wave of sexual honesty deprived Jayne of a persona. She couldn't sell her illicit appeal when the country had taken the sin out of sex.

A generation ten years younger than she had judged her. Never has an age group had so much power. Media and public relations people picked up on the dislikes of youth and Jayne was condemned to the glue factory. Jayne's style,

○ ○ ○ ○ ○ ○ ○ ○ ○ ○ ○ ○ ○ ○ ○ ○ ○ ○ ○ ○ ○ ○ ○ ○ ○ ○ ○ ○ ○ ○ ○ ○ ○ ○ ○ ○ ○ ○ ○ ○

mouthwatering in 1955, had become unpalatable in 1965. It wasn't so much that women became sexually or emotionally liberated in the sixties. It was that styles changed. When it turned out that good sex was the answer to a maiden's prayer, women, instead of learning how to say no, had to learn to say yes. With the Big O came the advent of a new anxiety rather than the alleviation of old ones. Sexual conquest, long familiar to men, became a game for women. Instead of being forced to be passive, chaste but provocative, women had to be aggressive, experimental and provocative. For women it was another side of the same old coin. And women barely got a cursory pit stop before they were expected to roar out in their new supercharged, fuel-injected sexuality.

Jayne never knew what hit her. One minute she'd been lisping and purring and making blue jokes at the Dunes and the next she was a has-been playing in rundown dives to dirty old men. In trying to accommodate herself to the new styles, she merely orchestrated all her sex-is-fun-because-it's-dirty training. Her decolletage went even lower, the jokes got even bluer and her act got, if possible, even more sex-kittenish and false.

Jayne caught fifties sex like a malignant fever and it burned her out with sixties complications. Sex, Jayne knew, had its volatile underside which lack of caution or understanding could activate. She thought she could handle it, but Jayne was never in charge. She didn't understand that excessive exposure to the fantasies of others would permanently change her. Like a child taking candy, she took the fun and attention her body provided. But she didn't control the exchange. She was the victim of how others saw her. She bought a picture of herself as a sexy, dumb broad in return for the thrill of turning men on. But, as they used to say in junior high school, they didn't respect her. She tried to ride the tiger of sexism and failed.

Jayne grappled with the insipid sexual mythology about

women, took it to its farthest perimeters. She thought she could triumph over the limitations of her assigned role and make it work for her, but because the definition wasn't hers to begin with, she lost herself.

The women's movement came too late to help. They might have applauded her courage and bravado, but they too would have denied her an identity. She is linked to feminism by a paradox. One hesitates to speculate on what Jayne might have said about women's liberation. And yet it's not such an odd combination — Jayne and the women's movement. She would have understood instinctively women's desires to achieve beyond the confines of a family, women challenging their traditional roles. And Jayne's outrageous, anarchic streak would have appreciated the imagination behind bra burnings and Miss America pickets. But without her sexual identity she was resourceless, and she and the movement would have collided head-on about sex.

As an uncertain feminist, I have found it hard at times to avoid moralizing or becoming self-righteous with Jayne. And yet, she must produce sympathy and compassion for the agonizing bind she found herself in. And her story must resonate with every woman who has ever felt used for her sexuality, who has ever been confused by the conflicting pressures of career and family, who has ever been tempted to use her sexuality for love, acceptance or gain, who has ever wanted more than she could have. Jayne's dilemma hounds all women who remember seeing the technical virgin of the fifties transmogrified into the raspberry-douching Cosmo girl of the sixties. It's almost impossible for me, as for Jayne, to make a coherent whole of those two symbols. One is almost required to cross one's eyes and let double vision replace the double standard.

In researching this book, I relied primarily on interviews and newspapers. Twentieth Century-Fox and its publicist, Jet Fore, helped immensely with details, pictures and screen-

○ ○ ○ ○ ○ ○ ○ ○ ○ ○ ○ ○ ○ ○ ○ ○ ○ ○ ○ ○ ○ ○ ○ ○ ○ ○ ○ ○ ○ ○ ○ ○ ○ ○ ○ ○ ○ ○ ○ ○

ings. I have also read two recent biographies which bear brief mention. *Jayne Mansfield, A Biography* by Las Vegas columnist May Mann is a singularly self-serving work in which the author cites a number of psychic encounters she presumably has had with Jayne since Jayne's death in 1967. On these occasions Jayne has urged Ms. Mann on in her endeavor, encouraging her to tell the whole truth. The truth, as revealed by Ms. Mann, is a series of increasingly sensational episodes interlaced with some occult observations. Ray Strait, a.k.a. Rusty Ray, has contributed to the literature *The Tragic Secret Life of Jayne Mansfield.* Strait was her underpaid press secretary for a number of years and elaborates at even greater length than May Mann on Jayne's sexual activities, including those with him. His most startling claim, ingeniously but not convincingly substantiated, is that Jayne had an affair with John Fitzgerald Kennedy. No one but Strait has any evidence of this, and since both parties are conveniently dead, the truth of the allegation will be forever in doubt. The suspicion remains, however, that Norman Mailer has unleashed a whole new variety of journalism on the world. Biographers now get to play posthumous musical beds with the brothers Kennedy and blond actresses. Both of these books were written by self-styled intimates and admirers of Jayne, and both are similarly bad tempered.

Unlike the memoirs of Jayne's friends, this is intended to be more and less than a biography. I have not included every extant piece of Mansfield material, because I didn't think her internal life sufficiently multifaceted to justify such detail. Jayne was not introspective, nor did she wish others to be. Perhaps I have done her an injustice, but I have treated her as a symbol, a phenomenon, a presence as much as a human being. I see her as a hinge between the fifties and sixties. In this context her personal dramas and disappointments are less distressing and more understandable.

○ ○ ○ ○ ○ ○ ○ ○ ○ ○ ○ ○ ○ ○ ○ ○ ○ ○ ○ ○ ○ ○ ○ ○ ○ ○ ○ ○ ○ ○ ○ ○ ○ ○ ○ ○ ○ ○ ○

People aren't theories, they aren't consistent, and they're often not rational. Jayne certainly was none of the above. But her life, like everyone's, was to some degree of her own making, the result of her own choices. The alternatives from which she chose, because they occurred at a certain time, were the alternatives open to a large group of women, her contemporaries. The forces which operated on Jayne operated on all women. Her response was to play out, with dreary and even tragic results, a role that remained a fantasy for nearly all other women. In some way she was the very real and inevitable conclusion of a blighted era.

# Jayne Mansfield and the American Fifties

# Vera's Dream

♥ ♥ ♥

AT FOUR A.M., June 29, 1967, a Texas state trooper knocked
on the door of an orchid-colored house in Dallas.  He woke
Vera and Harry Peers, apologizing for the hour saying,
"Mrs. Peers, I have some very bad news for you.  Your
daughter, Jayne Mansfield, has been in a very bad accident."

The trooper woke Vera from a nightmare, and, confused
and distraught as she was, she was not altogether surprised.  In the dream, "Jaynie was crying out to me, calling 'Mama, Mama,' or, 'Mama, come here.  I want you,
Mother.'  It woke me and I looked around.  It was that real.
I went back to sleep and in my dream Jaynie took me by
the hand.  She was smiling.  She was wearing a black hat
and so was I.  She said, 'I want you to be careful, Mama.
I'm going to help you down these steps.'  We were at the
top of some marble steps, beautiful stairs with doves and
cherubs carved in them.  There were hundreds of steps.
They were the heavenly stairs.  At the bottom there were
lots and lots of people and Jaynie said, 'Don't, worry,
Mama, I'm going to introduce you to these people.'  But I

○ ○ ○ ○ ○ ○ ○ ○ ○ ○ ○ ○ ○ ○ ○ ○ ○ ○ ○ ○ ○ ○ ○ ○ ○ ○ ○ ○ ○ ○ ○ ○ ○ ○ ○ ○ ○ ○ ○ ○

said, 'You don't have to. I'll know them when I see them.' "

Mrs. Peers believes that Jayne was telling her not to worry, that Jayne had already achieved the Kingdom of Heaven. Vera since has had the dream interpreted by portent-experts whose readings confirm hers.

Vera Peers is a small, gray-haired woman in her sixties, who favors red lipstick and trim navy knits. She wears her hair in what used to be called a bubble and protects it from the wind with a blue net hood. Vera's myopic brown eyes are set deep in a face which is still fetching. One minute she is girlish, winsome and giggly. The next moment the huge eyes behind the harlequin glasses cloud up with worry. She is as mercurial as a child. She feels, with some justification, that she has been through more in her lifetime than she deserves. "Too much has happened to me." She negotiates with the world through her husband, Harry, resident diplomat, interpreter, spokesman and guardian.

Harry is a tall, thin, weathered man, born in Fort Worth and educated at Texas A.&M. He has an old-fashioned graciousness and rarely raises his voice. His primary concern is Vera, to whom he refers as "Mama" or "Lover." He does everything humanly possible to see that she is not upset. The household turns on her moods. Harry deploys his dry, understated humor, his patience and his belief in the basically endearing frivolity of women to pacify Vera. She charms, amuses, baffles and frazzles him, but she never bores him. Vera depends on Harry's forbearance and stability, but he doesn't seem to interest her much.

The Peerses live in a tidy middle-class section of Dallas called University Park because of its proximity to Southern Methodist University. The purplish door of the one-story house opens on a formal living room carpeted in pink. Several white silk chairs and love seats stand at sharp

○ ○ ○ ○ ○ ○ ○ ○ ○ ○ ○ ○ ○ ○ ○ ○ ○ ○ ○ ○ ○ ○ ○ ○ ○ ○ ○ ○ ○ ○ ○ ○ ○ ○ ○ ○ ○

angles to each other. Two prominent portraits of Jayne
hang on the pink walls. In one, painted in Las Vegas,
Jayne is wearing a low-cut, dark green dress and a quantity
of deep red lipstick. The pose is serious and stilted, fea-
turing flashy highlights and fleshy tones. The blond hair
looks soft and the eyes look faraway. The other is an enormous photograph of a much more seductive, open-
mouthed Jayne, posed, touched and retouched in vintage
Hollywood.

The hallway adjacent to the living room is in effect a
Mansfield gallery including some of the laminated magazine covers on which she appeared. There are also some
studio shots of Jayne with Vera and Harry, with her children and with her second husband, the muscular Mickey
Hargitay. Two large stills of Jayne and Mickey at their
wedding reception hang in the living room. The unused
front room with the dead faithfully preserved has an atmosphere suitable to an embalming chamber.

Vera has covered the pink wall-to-wall carpeting with
white sheets because of Mike, the Peerses' miniature
poodle. Mike is an ill-mannered, hyperkinetic little creature with a red bow on his head and red toenails, touched
up weekly at the dog shampoo parlor. Vera often remarks
on how clean Mike is.

Beyond the pink room is a dining area with a table covered with dozens of three-by-two-foot scrapbooks filled
with Jayne's clippings, which it took Vera more than two
years to organize. Many of the clips are from European
magazines written in languages the Peerses can't read.
Vera designed the Styrofoam Valentine centerpiece on the
table. Cupids are shooting red pipe-cleaner arrows at
hearts decorated with particolored sequins. It conjures up
Jayne uncannily.

Mrs. Peers points out "the little girls' room," a pink
bathroom in heavy disguise. Groups of tiny, oval colored

lights hang grapelike from the ceiling. Next to the sink stand several containers for cosmetics, hand-decorated with ribbon glitter and net. A tall cylindrical receptacle done up as a pink felt poodle festooned with sequins holds pastel soap balls. The toilet is covered with layers of tutu-like gathered pink net secured by a large satin bow in the middle.

The Peerses do their real living in the long back room that looks out on a small patio where Harry's roses proliferate. Through the sliding doors you can see a statue of Jesus and a tiny fountain surrounded by low growing plants. The living room is subdued, done in tones of brown and dull orange, and has a large elevated fireplace equipped with a gas jet for lighting instant fires. Over a chair is a piece of framed needlepoint reading, "What we are is God's gift to us. What we become is our gift to God."

The sampler renders the individualist creed with which Jayne grew up. She bore the burden of proving herself. It was important that she *become* rather than just *be*. She justified her existence to God by becoming something, or in her case, really something. It could be said that she became what she was. She gave to God and as many millions of people as possible what God had given her.

The back room extends into the spot where a guesthouse used to stand. The Peerses built it some years ago to house Jayne and her entourage during her Dallas trips. The house seems lonely now, but Jayne's children often visit and disturb the quiet. The Peerses and their neighbors have recently taken to locking their doors carefully following the construction of several nearby apartment buildings bringing "a different element" to University Park.

Harry explains that "Mama is a little nervous." She hasn't recovered entirely from Jayne's death and she is worried about opening old wounds. "I can't believe it still," she says. She is anxious to see a book in which Jayne is considered favorably. There has been an enormous amount of sensational material which hasn't escaped her notice. Vera experiences pain more intensely than most. Jayne was her only child and the central emotional moment of her life.

She naturally prefers not to look too closely at some aspects of Jayne's life. Vagueness helps her avoid pain. She can't date occurrences. "I don't think of the time. I never associate age and time. I never do. Just like when I lost my mother and father. I didn't want to remember when. I just knew it happened sometime. That's the way I am with everything, you know." Vera is also anxious to preserve her good relations with her grandchildren, which an incautious word could jeopardize.

She begins. Vera Jeffrey met Herbert Palmer in Pen Argyl, Pennsylvania, north of Bethlehem. They went to the same Methodist church and the same high school. Vera started teaching kindergarten at eighteen and taught until she married Herbert in her early twenties. Palmer was an aggressive young lawyer, a graduate of Lehigh University where he had been the drum major of the marching band. The young couple moved to nearby Phillipsburg, where Palmer set up practice. He was a handsome blond and exceedingly ambitious. He was also a "natural musician and played the accordion and violin."

Vera was extremely anxious to have children. She became pregnant and carried a child, a son, almost ten months. At the time of his delivery the doctors told Vera's mother that either Vera or the child would survive but not both. Mrs. Jeffrey chose her daughter. Vera was told later that she would have had a strikingly beautiful boy. It took Vera a long time to recover from the unfortunate pregnancy.

In time, however, she became pregnant again. "I was

o o o o o o o o o o o o o o o o o o o o o o o o o o o o o o o o o o o o

obsessed with having a child." She took great precautions
during her term and finally went into a hospital in Bryn
Mawr. Vera Jayne Palmer was born by Caesarean section
on April 19, 1933, weighing 9 lbs. 10 oz. The doctors antic-
ipated a long recuperation for the mother, but Vera was too
happy to languish.

Jayne was an easy baby to be with and easy to mother.
Vera's later relations with Jayne were prefigured in her
birth. Vera was a devoted, careful, protective mother, ut-
terly engrossed in her daughter. Jayne was the only child
she could have and came in for more than her share of attention, some loving and some critical. Vera held Jayne in
a tender half nelson as long as she could. Both her parents
wanted Jayne desperately, and that primitive security gave
Jayne a confidence that rarely deserted her.

The Palmers lived in a small white frame house in Phillipsburg. Jayne's relation with Herbert was loving and
playful. He played with her long brown hair and generally
indulged his pretty, affectionate daughter. Before Jayne
was in school, Herbert bought her a Shirley Temple song-
book, which Vera still keeps. Vera and Jayne learned all
her songs and went to all her movies. Shirley Temple emphasized the child in Vera and reduced her and Jayne to
equals. The little star made a strong impression on Jayne.
She later said, "I always knew I'd be just as big as Shirley
Temple. She was my ideal. From the moment I saw her
movies, I knew I was going to be a big star too."

After Herbert brought home the book, Vera recalls,
"Friends used to say to me, 'Well, look out, Vera, she *is*
adorable and look out what she is going to do. She seems
made for that, you know.' I think there was something in
my background I passed on to her. I was just good at acting. It just came natural. Jaynie was just always theatrically minded. When she'd go to the movies she would

○ ○ ○ ○ ○ ○ ○ ○ ○ ○ ○ ○ ○ ○ ○ ○ ○ ○ ○ ○ ○ ○ ○ ○ ○ ○ ○ ○ ○ ○ ○ ○ ○ ○ ○ ○ ○ ○

*drink* it in. There was *no fooling*. She would follow *every-thing*." Vera likes to take responsibility for Jayne's devotion to Shirley Temple and the movies. "I used to promise her if she was a good little girl we'd go to the movies and she could have chewing gum, lollipops and ice cream. And you know, I might have instilled something in her at that tender age." Vera's theatrical bent is evident. She tells a story with pauses, eye rolling, forefinger shaking, voice dropping and weighty repetitions. She sometimes sacrifices accuracy to drama, but it's certainly entertainment.

Hundreds of thousands of girls were raised on the Shirley Temple diet, but most of them survived. Jayne, however, with her mother's enthusiastic cooperation, spent her life trying to incorporate that saccharine, precocious, little ringletted fantasy into her grown-up, obvious, big-busted self. Jayne learned very early that little girls are a mixed metaphor for sexuality. Sex in the fifties required a lecherous male and a childlike female. Jayne aped Shirley Temple's innocence and wound up acting like jailbait. In a culture that has only recently placed any value on sexually mature women, the obvious side effect of Shirley Temple worship is Lance Rentzel.

While Vera and Jayne were absorbing Shirley Temple, Herbert was pursuing his law career vigorously. He had become friends with Robert Meyner, later governor of New Jersey. One evening he sat down with Vera and said, "I'm going into politics. I want to be President." Vera said that had he been anyone else she would have shrugged it off, but she believed in him and his capabilities, although the intensity of his ambition frightened her. In 1935 he entered the Warren County race for Republican assemblyman. He lost the election but had big plans for an upcoming contest.

o o o o o o o o o o o o o o o o o o o o o o o o o o o o o o o o o o o o o

He never had the chance to try his luck. When Jayne was three, she, her mother and father had crossed the Delaware River and were driving up a hill to Easton, Pennsylvania. Suddenly, Herbert slumped over the wheel. Vera maneuvered the car to the side of the road. By the time she got him to a hospital Herbert Palmer was dead of a heart attack.

Jayne, who has been described as "having the strongest career drive of anyone in show business," must have inherited some of that quality from her father. Her ambition moved her toward Hollywood, the woman's equivalent of the White House.

It's hard to estimate the effect Herbert Palmer's death had on his daughter, but it does seem that his early demise bears some relation to her constant search for male attention and approval. She had an apparently boundless need for men. Her lawyer, Greg Bautzer, says, "She was like Will Rogers. She never met a man she didn't like." Whether what she felt can be called liking, need or desperation, everyone agrees that men were the focus of her life. She described her career as a campaign to win over all the men in the country. It would be a wild oversimplification to attribute Jayne's attempted national seduction to the loss of her father. But young children usually interpret the death of a parent as a desertion and some of Jayne was always compensating for that void.

Harry Peers was working for Ingersoll-Rand in Phillipsburg when he met Vera. After she was widowed, Vera's family wanted her to stay single, to throw herself on a kind of latter-day suttee for Herbert. Her minister, however, disagreed and advised her to remarry and start over again. Harry found Vera very beautiful and appealing in her distress.

"They do things different now, you know," says Vera, reflecting on the slow, courtly way she and Harry came to marry. They were married in St. Louis in 1939. St. Louis, Harry explains, because it was halfway between Phillipsburg and Harry's home in Dallas.

Vera took a train back to Phillipsburg after the wedding to collect Jayne and take her to Dallas. On the train, a man importuned Vera with disagreeable advances. She reported his behavior to the conductor who deposited the offender on some plain between St. Louis and Phillipsburg. Harry says with admiration, "He just picked the fellow up by the scruff of the neck and threw him off the train. It's different now. That wouldn't happen." Neither Vera nor Harry is quite comfortable in a world in which the conductor no longer controls his own train.

The Peerses categorize activity which they don't understand under the rubric of Things Being Different Now. Much of Jayne's behavior comes under this classification. The phrase is slightly misleading insofar as it implies at least an uneasy acceptance of things new and troubling. Neither Harry nor Vera is noticeably easygoing or tolerant. Vera never said to Jayne, single, sixteen and pregnant, "Well, you know, things are different now." But over the years of difficulties, the Peerses have resigned themselves to operating with less than the personal and social control they were raised to expect.

Vera and Jayne arrived in Dallas in the summer of 1939. Vera still remembers the paralyzing heat of those first unair-conditioned summers. Harry recalls Vera's first night in Dallas. They were lying in bed and Vera wanted to know where the cowboys and Indians were. Harry says with his beguiling smile, "Now I would have expected that from Jaynie, but not Vera." The recollection tickles Harry whose world is peopled with sweet, wilting, uninformed women. He supports them, protects them and treats them with limitless courtesy. Women are not to work. Vera, he says, has her hands full taking care of him and the de-

∘ ∘ ∘ ∘ ∘ ∘ ∘ ∘ ∘ ∘ ∘ ∘ ∘ ∘ ∘ ∘ ∘ ∘ ∘ ∘ ∘ ∘ ∘ ∘ ∘ ∘ ∘ ∘ ∘ ∘ ∘ ∘ ∘ ∘ ∘ ∘ ∘ ∘

manding poodle. Yes, she had been teaching until they married, but that was *before*. Marriage made her his charge and he takes complete responsibility for her. He is still appalled, not only that Jayne worked, but also that her husbands shared her earnings. He thinks that makes them less than men, but quickly adds, "they have different values." Some years ago, Harry continues, Vera wanted to go back to work. She got a job at a neighborhood department store where she received a small salary and a 20 percent discount on the store's merchandise. Harry says, with his continual indulgent smile, that Vera's six months at work cost him between six and seven thousand dollars. Vera, amused in spite of herself, remonstrates playfully, "Oh, Harry." "That's right, Lover," he says. "You've got plenty to do what with me and Mike."

As a small girl, Jayne observed Harry's gentle, relentless paternalism. Jayne knew the full gale force of her mother's personality, knew that she wasn't the helpless, weak, fluttery woman whom Harry chose to see. She knew a critical, possessive and powerful mother. On the other hand, she knew instinctively that Harry liked, approved of and needed his own version of Vera. As she grew up, Jayne looked at herself through Harry's eyes, judged herself by his criteria and parlayed his vision into one of the country's all-time dingy, useless, bean-brained broads. She knew it was an act, she knew Vera and Harry both profited by it and she knew it worked.

The first time Harry met Jayne, she was about three "and had the vocabulary of a twelve-year-old." She was very verbal, loved word games and did well in school. Harry says, "She worked but she never had to, you know." She excelled in languages, Spanish, French and English.

Teachers remember Jayne as a good student and exceptionally well behaved. She was a modest girl, if not shy, not an attention seeker either. "Well brought up" is their opinion. Although an only child, she was never lonely, Vera says emphatically. She was choosy about her friends and loyal to the chosen. Since she was precocious she got along well with the Peerses' circle. Vera says she was never afraid of anyone.

Mrs. Peers is an observant Methodist, has been all her life. Jayne, she says firmly, was very religious. Jayne's spiritual life resembled Harry's more than her mother's. He said, "I was raised a Catholic, but when I was a young boy my mother told me to pick my church. I went to many churches, but never felt I'd found the right one. I didn't think it mattered very much. I always thought that if you lived as a good man during the week and went to any church on Sunday that was right. When Jaynie was a little girl, I took her around to various churches with me. She felt closest to the Catholic Church. She loved the ceremony and the incense. She finally converted when she moved to Los Angeles."

In fact, Jayne never did convert to Catholicism, although she sometimes wanted to. She attended All Saints Episcopal, a very posh Beverly Hills Church, but never joined because she had been divorced. Her second marriage to a Greek Orthodox Hungarian took place in a Swedenborgian chapel. Later she toyed with the idea of becoming a Jew, how seriously it's hard to tell. Jayne's life was remarkably ecumenical thanks to Harry's early example and the company she kept. In the end, she was rather more ecumenical than her mother, who uses the word "nigger," was prepared for.

Vera's Jaynie was an innocent, ethical child. "She never stole a cent the way other children sometimes do. And she always believed other people were honest the same way. Maybe I raised her wrong." Vera remembers with bitter-

ness Jayne's later financial embroilments and her own ex-
clusion from the large estate Jayne left.

Money is very important to the Peerses. Harry points
out that one of his commissions from the sale of Ingersoll-
Rand's heavy equipment is plenty for them to live well for
many months. They own their house in Dallas and a
house in Colorado. As their third and final son-in-law,
Matt Cimber, ungraciously put it, "They have the first dollar they ever earned." Comfortable as they are, they don't
like to spend money, worry about it and are well informed
about the cost of everything. Next to Mike, prices domi-
nate the Peerses' conversation. Vera doesn't buy her favorite Godiva chocolates at Neiman-Marcus anymore because they cost too much. Harry and Vera share a kind of
unloving tightness, an unwillingness to treat themselves
well, which, of course, affected Jayne. Her stinginess was
legendary and she died remarkably rich.

Jayne began promoting freebies at an early age. In 1945,
when she was twelve, Vera remembers, ". . . we had three
puppies—and she heard on the radio, Swan Soap offered
'free soap for your new baby.' Soap was rationed. Un-
known to us, Jayne wrote Swan Soap she had triplets,
Sammy, Pammy and Jammy." Lever Brothers wrote "Mrs.
Vera Palmer" a congratulatory letter and sent her a case of
Swan Soap.

Harry laughs and says, "She was very extravagant. She
wouldn't spend a penny on a stick of gum, but she'd go
out and spend four hundred dollars on a car or a television
set." She worked at odd jobs to make enough money for
her first car, a red Buick which she bought in 1953. It still
gives Harry a kick to remember that she wouldn't spend
thirty-five cents for a car wash, preferring to spend her Sat-
urdays scrubbing the Buick. Conspicuous consumption
was a characteristic of Jayne and the era. Later Jayne was

willing to buy, if she couldn't promote, clothes, jewels, furs, houses and cars, things which could be seen and envied. But she never wanted to spend a nickel on invisible or impermanent things like travel, food, tips or salaries.

While Jayne was promoting soap, she was deep into the movies. She read every fan magazine available and covered her entire bedroom with photographs of stars. Always a sucker for brawn, her favorite actor was Johnny Weissmuller. Jayne did such a thorough decorating job that Vera "had to have it all redone." Vera doesn't think Jayne's obsession with Hollywood was unusual. "Don't you think all teen-agers are interested in the movies? Some are more than others. And Jaynie was. She was just theatrically inclined."

Vera is right, of course. Teen-agers who grew up in the late forties and early fifties were almost universally fascinated with Hollywood. Studio publicity departments were in their salad days cranking out romance and splendor, protecting the fans from the dreadful knowledge that stars have nervous breakdowns, fallen arches and parents too. It takes more than a studio to sustain an illusion, and the country was willing, after the war, to play its part in deifying Hollywood. Stars manifestly led perfect lives. And what fourteen-year-old never imagined herself discovered in Schwab's Drugstore?

Even at her most famous, Jayne never lost her starry-eyed feeling about Hollywood. Against the advice of all her friends, agents and counselors, she made a vapid, ill-advised movie called *Kiss Them For Me,* because she wanted the chance to work with Cary Grant. The Hollywood version of the American Dream, from which Jayne never awoke, was merely an advanced form of a girl's reverie in which the most popular boy at school asks her to dance. Class president or producer, the girl was always

o o o o o o o o o o o o o o o o o o o o o o o o o o o o o o o o o o o o o

waiting.  But Jayne couldn't wait, and her impatience had as much to do with her successes as it did with her failures.

Vera and Harry hold on for dear life to a simple, downhome Jayne.  They remember the little girl who always liked everything homemade, clothes and cookies, who was always saying, "Now, Mama, I don't want store-bought brownies."  Little Jaynie brought home stray and maimed dogs and nursed them back to life.  She inundated her parents with pets.  Her favorite job was working in a veterinary hospital.  Vera has always thought Jayne would have been happiest married to a farmer.  "She would have had clean air, modern conveniences, lovely music, television, and all those animals."

# Class of 1950

♥  ♥  ♥

JAYNE HAD two "best friends" in high school. Ann Wedgeworth is a tall, slender, beautiful actress now in her early
forties. She has long, tangled black hair, deep-set dark eyes
and pale skin. She looks bruised but it's an illusion
created by her pallor and uncertain demeanor. She talks
slowly and softly in a West Texas drawl and says very little.
She is nervous, smokes a lot and appears preoccupied.
She has appeared in *Scarecrow* and *Bang the Drum Slowly*
and stars in *Law and Disorder*. Ann lives on the West Side of
New York in a chaotic apartment. There is a platoon of
strollers lined up in the hallway, a playpen in the middle of
the living room, dolls, plastic balls, rattles, blankets and
toys covering every surface. A miniature dog with a plastic barrette in her hair darts around the room. Highland
Park High she says with some feeling "was a real snob
school."

Charlsa Feinstein, née Wolf, is an energetic, talkative
woman who lives in Phoenix. She met Jayne when they
were fifteen, sophomores at Highland Park. Charlsa came
from a much more prosperous family than Ann and her

o o o o o o o o o o o o o o o o o o o o o o o o o o o o o o o o o o o o o o o o

view of Highland Park High is somewhat different. "Highland Park is a section of Dallas that's considered the best section of town. I don't think there were any colored students at all because I'm not sure that they sold homes to any Negroes in that whole area. It was kind of a separate place, it was kind of an unwritten rule, so we did not have what you'd call a *cross section* in our high school. It was upper-class and upper-middle-class. They were *not* blue-collar workers."

Charlsa goes on about the atmosphere. "We didn't know what was going on in the outside world, or did we care. We didn't think about civil rights, we were thinking about what we were going to do this weekend. The biggest thing in our life was to learn to drive."

The period was in many ways less complicated than it became for subsequent adolescents. Jayne's primary relations were with her parents and her school. She was not obliged to take an interest in anything beyond these perimeters. High school has since become less pivotal, or rather, an experience greatly tempered by all kinds of input. In 1950 what television was available to Jayne was very limited. She grew up before *Sputnik*, McCarthy, MacArthur, Checkers, Kennedy, Vietnam, Martin Luther King, Watergate, before, in other words the sluice gates of the media opened and deluged the public with a torrent of facts, scares and counterscares.

In Jayne's class girls got manicures and had their hair done. They performed Toni home permanents on each other. They wore short-sleeve sweaters and Peter Pan blouses. They wore straight skirts or circular skirts with hundreds of crinolines and wide elastic belts. They wore ballerina-length formals and armpit-length gloves, or those slipcovers for the arm which hook over the thumb but don't cover the fingers. They wore loafers and white socks. They wore girdles to hold in their tiny stomachs

○ ○ ○ ○ ○ ○ ○ ○ ○ ○ ○ ○ ○ ○ ○ ○ ○ ○ ○ ○ ○ ○ ○ ○ ○ ○ ○ ○ ○ ○ ○ ○ ○ ○ ○ ○ ○ ○ ○

because Amy Vanderbilt warned that the smallest bulge could ruin the line of a skirt. They wore uplift bras designed to make breasts look like phototropic ice cream cones at 10:00 A.M. They pulled the straps up as far as possible, making their shoulders sore with red indentations. In short, girls had plenty to think about without resorting to foreign affairs or inflation.

Ann met Jayne when they were fourteen. "She was very friendly. She was very sweet and we neither one of us had a lot of friends. It was a very very cliquey school. Jaynie was very goodhearted."

Charlsa's first impression of Jayne was "Real pretty. She was *awful* pretty. *Sweet* person. She was always smiling. She was never nervous. At that time she was very good for me because I tended to be nervous." On second thought, Charlsa says she was pretty "but she wasn't that out*standing*. She was not a *gorgeous* creature. She always had a good figure and I think she was always conscious of that fact and she would wear things that emphasized her figure."

Jayne was a wholesome-looking brunette with hazel eyes and great teeth. She wore her hair in a short pageboy with bangs. Her face, while pleasant, was never her strong point. She wore dark red lipstick, maybe Revlon's Rosy Future, and, like all teen-agers in the fifties, looked at least ten years older than she was. It was a time when it still seemed desirable to grow up.

Jayne was a reasonable student. She maintained a respectable B average and was particularly good in Spanish. Charlsa says, "It used to drive me crazy because I thought everybody should *hate* their foreign language." Ann says with reverence if not accuracy, "She was very smart. She always made A's."

"Basically she was an innately bright person," Charlsa continues. "We figured things out pretty well. She

○ ○ ○ ○ ○ ○ ○ ○ ○ ○ ○ ○ ○ ○ ○ ○ ○ ○ ○ ○ ○ ○ ○ ○ ○ ○ ○ ○ ○ ○ ○ ○ ○ ○ ○ ○ ○ ○ ○

wanted to do well for her mother." Jayne wasn't interested in schoolwork for its own sake but as a means to other things. She wanted to keep Vera happy. And Vera supplied her with practical motivations for achievement. Jayne brought home a low geometry grade and wanted to go horseback riding. Vera made the ride contingent on a 100 percent geometry exam. Jayne showed up with a perfect test and got her ride.

Jayne played in the school orchestra, "the last violin or something," Charlsa says. Both Jayne and her mother were proud of her musical ability and Vera still thinks Jayne could have had a great musical career. Jayne was a member of the school horseback-riding club and was interested in drama.

She was disappointed in her efforts to join the drama club. Charlsa, who was a member, recalls, "This woman that was the head of this thing wouldn't let her in. She didn't pass the test or something. She wanted to be in it and I think that probably was one of the things that spurred her on later. To show them. There was no real reason for it, because she was as good as anybody else I can remember sitting there."

Charlsa and Jayne and Ann talked and giggled together in the tradition of best friends. "Lord only knows what we talked about," says Charlsa, "but it was things like boys, school, teachers, horses, dogs. You know, stuff that fifteen-year-old girls talk about. Not particularly dates because neither of us went out that much.

"I remember Mrs. Peers took us one year to the Neiman-Marcus fashion show, the big fall back-to-school show. I remember sitting there with her mother looking at clothes and her mother saying, 'Now, you girls have got to lose some weight if you're going to look like that.'

"Because we both of us just *adored* eating. And we were both a bit *zoftig*. She would come over to our house and mother would buy tons of fruit, and we would set in the bowl six peaches and a whole thing of cherries and Lord only knows what else and we would take it up to my room. We would sit up all night and eat this fruit. In the morning there'd be a bunch of seeds.

"Or like at three o'clock in the morning we'd get up and we'd decide that we wanted to make fudge. People don't do that anymore, they're thinking about diets."

Jayne's social life in high school was unexceptional, at least in the beginning. It does not conform to her own version of it to Jim Bishop in 1957 in the *American Weekly* in which she claimed to have started dating at eleven, having matured physically very early and attracted lots of male attention.

Vera gets defensive about Jayne's social life. "Well, now look, she was a homebody. She just went to several girls' houses, that's all. She didn't start dating at an early age, did she?"

"No," replies Harry, "she preferred to be home or seeing her girl friends."

Jayne was a homebody largely because she was something of a wallflower. Charlsa says, "She really was not popular in high school. She really didn't have a lot of dates, and the dates she had were with kind of tacky fellows, nothing really great and few and far between. We would talk about these guys and we decided they were really *dumb*, but I mean, she had to go to a dance so that was the only way.

"We would sleep over at each other's houses. She loved to sleep at my house because I lived in a neighborhood with lots of boys. My mother had gotten me a Ping-Pong table, so after dinner we would go outside and play Ping-Pong and the kids from all over the neighborhood would come over. There must have been about six or seven boys and a couple of girls. Then about nine, ten at night we'd all pile into someone's car and go downtown and get a root beer."

Charlsa remembers one of Jayne's boyfriends. "There was a guy she was crazy about that was a bus boy at a restaurant. I remember dragging my family to the restaurant to take a look at him. I said, '*Mother,* that's *him.*' 'That's who?' 'That is the guy Jaynie's crazy about.' 'A *bus* boy?' she said.

"He did have a car. That was a selling point. I don't remember how long he lasted, not too long, but I remember he did take a bunch of us to see a radio show called the *U.S. Steel Hour.* It came to Dallas for one performance, so this guy took us out to Fair Park to see this thing. Of course, we were madly in love with the actors. Jayne was crazy about John Lund and I was crazy about Richard Widmark. I think maybe we were crazy about them because they were there."

Jayne mentioned another of her boyfriends in a curious and touching letter she wrote to her parents one day from study hall. The letter is largely an encomium to them, "the best parents in the whole world." She hoped they would be proud of her grades and also hoped that they would like "Buddy." She liked him very much and thought he was very handsome.

Vera doesn't remember Buddy or that Jayne dated at all. "I took good care of her, you know. I went for her every day of her life and met her so that I would see that she wouldn't get into anything that she shouldn't, you know. Because she was a very beautiful girl and I thought, well, I don't want any boys hanging around that shouldn't. I was there in the car waiting for her every day after high school." The Peerses lived a long way from Highland Park High and it was a tedious drive for Vera.

Harry used to drop Jayne off on his way to work in the

morning. "We always knew where she was," Vera says chillingly.

Charlsa's view of Jayne's relations with her parents doesn't jibe exactly with Jayne's later descriptions. Charlsa says, "Oh, they *adored* her, just loved her. They adored Jaynie, anything that she used to do. They thought she was just *great.*"

Ann agrees. "Her mother thought Jayne was adorable. Just precious. Jaynie never complained about them."

Charlsa adds, "Jaynie wanted to please her mother very much, I mean she was her mother. I think her mother always set high standards for her. It was a rather middle-class household she came from, with rather strict morals, maybe almost too strict for her."

In later years Jayne was to blame her mother for being too critical, too severe and not loving enough. And yet their closeness persisted. There is no doubt that Vera was devoted to Jayne. She still has a white-hot admiration for her daughter, a need to convert people to Jaynie-worship. And she put the fear of God into Jayne. Jayne ran from the highly moralistic atmosphere of the house, but she never got away clean. Throughout her life she maintained an uneasy kind of dualism provoked by her opposing convictions that her mother was right and wrong.

Jayne played out this dialectic all her life. She preached Vera's morality and acted with a guilty kind of license. She slept around less for the sensual fun of it than for "love." One can be skeptical about the depth of meaning which attaches to the word "love." Jayne was probably as in love with John Lund as with her first husband. It was a high school word and a high school feeling, learned largely from the movies. But for all of that, it had a naiveté and a genuine, if shallow passion which was both sweet and innocent. It's certainly dying out among adolescents, but it beat everything in 1950. Romance, of course, was the first casualty of the new sexuality. Jayne struggled with increasing desperation, as she grew older, to hang onto her high school romanticism.

From the beginning Jayne was always in love. Her affection was abundant and incautious and she dispensed it generously. This trait worried Vera enormously. She was far more cynical about her daughter's swains than Jayne ever became.

Romance at Highland Park High involved willing self-deception. Jayne had crushes on boys she knew were "dumb," but the feeling obliterated realism. She, Charlsa and Ann sat around listening to "Stardust" and encouraged each other to overlook the shortcomingings exhibited by the available males. Instead, they turned decent, average, uninspired adolescents into monsters of perfection, men who walked tall, had exotic talents and unbridled passions. It was often hard to work from the materials at hand, but the fantasies flourished in inverse proportion to the accessibility of the subject.

Since Jayne was not notably popular, she was in an ideal position to cultivate a hearty garden of romantic daydreams. Ann said wistfully, "There was the in group and we were out. That bothered her some. That may have been part of the thing that gave her the push later — to show them."

Very popular girls were always shrewder than marginally successful ones. They were more realistic, which was partly a reason for their success and partly a result of it. Clear assessment of their objective aided them in selecting the appropriate weapons for the hunt. The ability to seem nonchalant was a devastating technique, one generally not available to the more romantically inclined girls. Girls like Jayne found it hard to hide their interest and were either avoided or exploited for it.

Unfortunately for Jayne, success in high school depended far more on that mysterious ingredient, personality, than it did on physical charms. "She's not so pretty,"
they used to say, "but she has a great personality." There
seems to have been one quintessential personality, a sort of
pan-personality which was good for all American high
schools for a period of some fifteen years. The vocabulary
changed and the rituals differed, but a girl could be assured of popularity if she'd been blessed with the personality gene.

Those who didn't have personality still find it eludes definition. Outwardly the traits included effortless and amus-
ing conversation, slight but not threatening bravado, perfect timing, physical sureness and grace, dry palms,
light-colored hair and a tendency to plumpness.

The signal feature lacking in the true personality girl was
any visible sign of sexuality. She was clean, wholesome
and sexless. Down below in the hierarchy was her coun-
terpart, the girl who was popular because she put out. She
was hopelessly tainted. Girls gossiped about her in the
lavatory. She was cheap, she had a bad reputation. Boys
only took her out for *that*. They didn't respect her. It was
cosmically shocking when one of the personality girls got
knocked up. The bargain seemed to be that they could
function on a sexless plain because they were, quite simply, terrific.

The personality burden on a teen-age girl was unspeak-
ably heavy. It was perhaps the major adolescent differen-
tiation between boys and girls. Boys were encouraged to
develop interests, achieve, learn and plan for their futures.
Girls relied on some nebulous combination of wits and
looks to get appreciated. While boys made projects for the
science fair girls went to charm school. But inevitably the
girl who had to resort to lessons was a born loser. Cruel
exploiters of the losers taught them to walk with books on

○ ○ ○ ○ ○ ○ ○ ○ ○ ○ ○ ○ ○ ○ ○ ○ ○ ○ ○ ○ ○ ○ ○ ○ ○ ○ ○ ○ ○ ○ ○ ○ ○ ○ ○ ○ ○ ○ ○ ○ ○ ○

their heads and write thank-you notes, but good posture never got anybody a date. The dreadful truth was that you either had it or you didn't. The nonelect read columns about how to converse with boys. Get him to talk. Know what a carburetor is. Ask him about Duke Snider's batting average. Let him open the door for you. Read a newspaper. The homemade personality was a study in double guessing the opposition. It was necessarily reactive and secondary. The ideal was to be enthusiastic, cheerful, interested and responsive. The real personality girl was assured that she conformed to boys' fantasies. Lacking that assurance, a girl devoted herself to worrying about what pose to adopt, what voice to use to approximate what she thought he thought she should sound like. And how far she should go.

High school was one apprenticeship; home was another. Popularity in school demanded things of Jayne which ran counter to Vera's rule. Jayne tried hard to please her mother with good grades, good nature and acquiescence, but the call-of-the-wild social life was louder than the Peerses' moralizing. So Jayne, failing personality, fell back on sex in an effort to please the other peers. At home, she couldn't do enough to get the acceptance and love she needed, so she went after it elsewhere.

The personality girl strung along all the most desirable boys. That was the greatest achievement life held out to any female. The nonelect ensnared the lame and the halt, the slide-rule carriers, wonks and nurds, the boys who wore white socks and reindeer sweaters.

Small wonder that Jayne's ambition, formed in high school, should stem from the personality principle. Her desire to attract a letterman escalated to attract all men, lettered or un. Jayne spend the better part of her life trying various arrangements and rearrangements of traits hoping to light on the final personality. For Jayne, as for most

o o o o o o o o o o o o o o o o o o o o o o o o o o o o o o o o o o o o o o

females, it was her only marketable quality. High school was a kind of bush-league training camp preparing her for the big-league personality series. Her talent as an adult performer had as limited success as her personality in high school, so, once again, she fell back on putting out.

"She did have," Charlsa says reflectively, "a rather normal childhood growing up in Dallas."

# A Teen-Ager in Love

♥ ♥ ♥

JAYNE USED to say about her first husband, "Paul was twenty and the handsomest boy in our crowd. He was a terrific party boy and had the most beautiful eyes. I think I married him for his eyes. So nine and a half months later I had a little baby girl." Sometimes she cited Paul's piano playing and his skill as a raconteur as reasons for the marriage.

Paul Mansfield went to nearby Sunset High School in Oak Cliff. Harry says he was "a bit of a showoff." Vera recalls Paul's most endearing trait. "He used to sing to her over the phone. He'd sing all the modern songs over the phone by the hour. I used to say, 'Jaynie, I have to use the phone,' but she'd say, 'Don't interrupt me now, Paul's singing this song,' you know, whatever the song of the time was. He was all right, you know. Paul's nice."

When asked why Jayne and Paul got married so young, Harry laughs benevolently and asks, "Why do kids do it?"

May Mann gives a sensational account of the wedding in *Jayne Mansfield, A Biography.* According to Ms. Mann,

○ ○ ○ ○ ○ ○ ○ ○ ○ ○ ○ ○ ○ ○ ○ ○ ○ ○ ○ ○ ○ ○ ○ ○ ○ ○ ○ ○ ○ ○ ○ ○

Jayne said that when she was fourteen (after 1960, Jayne persistently scraped years off her life) she had gone to a party where she'd been fed a concoction of fruit juice and vodka. She passed out and woke up pregnant. She immediately started looking around for a husband and chose Paul, comely, decent and unremarkable. He never quite knew what hit him. The two were secretly married two weeks later. Jayne continued to live at home until she could no longer conceal her pregnancy. At that point she and her mother had one of those "You have ruined your life, you have ruined my life" scenes, but Vera finally came around and gave the couple a small wedding.

Charlsa remembers a less melodramatic story. Jayne met Paul through a friend and thought he was "handsome and gorgeous." Charlsa gave a party and Paul showed up. She asked Jayne about him, and she said, "Oh, I think he's just *gorgeous,* and I invited him to come. I hope you don't mind."

The only snag in the affair was that Paul had brought a date, "a woman who looked like she was much older than any of us. She had a hat on. She was a working girl. Looking back she could have been maybe twenty, but she looked *ancient*." Jayne was sixteen and wearing a ballerina dress.

"Jaynie, she was just panting because he really *came.* He brought this date, but then that was okay. He stayed a few minutes and I sized him up. My impression of him at the time was, 'Jaynie, he's too old for you, he's too experienced for you. He's not right.' "

But, as Ann Wedgeworth said quietly, "Jaynie was crazy about him."

"He was with the Sunset Quartet or something," Charlsa continued. "That was one of the selling points of Paul. She thought he could sing anything. You know he was so glamorous. In fact, one of the things that just completely

won her over was the fact that he got his quartet to come
over and serenade her. That just did it. She was putty in
his hands from then on out." So, through a combination
of ignorance and bliss, Jayne became pregnant.

Charlsa heard about it from Paul when she was a freshman at the University of Texas. "I just collapsed. I felt
like her mother. Sixteen years old, she hadn't even graduated from *high* school yet. She went on and graduated
from high school and didn't tell anybody. This jerk gets
up and announces it to the whole class, at the country club
after graduation. He gets up and says, 'We are married
now and we are going to have a baby.' I didn't know
whether Jaynie liked it or not, but anyway she was stuck
with it. She accepted congratulations all evening.

"That killed her mother, you know, that really did because Jaynie had her whole life ahead of her. She was so
young. That really just killed her.

"I don't think she should have gotten married then. At
sixteen she was not prepared for marriage. She should
never have married him, that's all there was to it. There
were things, I suppose that could have been done, even in
those days. It wasn't the Middle Ages."

Jayne was an unworldly sixteen. Like most girls, her
concept of marriage didn't go much beyond the ceremony.
She had a high school friend who'd just run off and married a freshman at Southern Methodist University. He
used to come to the Highland Park High cafeteria to have
lunch with his "wife." The bride talked about her "husband" and "married life." To Jayne, it was, says Charlsa,
"the greatest thing, the end of the world." Jayne's imagination lingered over the tingle of excitement she felt saying
those new words to herself. Being secretly married, and to
a college man (Paul was at the university in Austin), tickled
her sense of adventure. In the context of her high school
life, Paul was very mysterious and desirable. She naturally

acquired some of that mystery by marrying him, and she became, in her own eyes, a far more interesting and daring girl.

The Peerses' strictness about Jayne's social life heightened Paul's attraction. They didn't approve of Jayne going out with someone older. Fantasies flourish under repression, and the Peerses, unwittingly, helped Jayne leap into Paul's arms. Paul had a certain amount of razzle-dazzle in the eyes of a sixteen-year-old, but his razzle-dazzle quotient skyrocketed when he was rationed.

Jayne and Paul were married in Fort Worth on May 6, 1950, and Jayne Marie Mansfield was born in November of that year. Vera relented and gave the couple a party after graduation. Ann, who spent most of her time in the kitchen because she was shy, remembers Paul playing the piano and singing. Paul went to Austin that fall, but Jayne stayed in Dallas to wait for the baby.

When the time came, the Peerses took Jayne to St. Paul's, a large Catholic hospital. Vera was quite beside herself, weeping throughout Jayne's long labor. The mother superior was only supposed to allow husbands to wait, so she threw the Peerses out. They sneaked back in. Their family physician found them and let them stay provided Vera stop crying. Labor was extended but the delivery was easy and Jayne was out of the hospital in relatively short order.

Jayne planned to go to the university with Paul. "I just had to go to college," she said. "I mean — what could I ever say to my children if they asked, 'Mommie, where did *you* go to college?'"

Jayne's attitude about education never developed beyond the utilitarian. A good geometry grade equaled horseback riding. IQs were fashionable in the fifties and Jayne assigned herself a good-sized one. She talked about it a lot, usually in contexts like, "Nobody cares about a figure like 163; they're more interested in 40-21-35. Even a

o o o o o o o o o o o o o o o o o o o o o o o o o o o o o o o o o o o o o o o o o

dumb blonde like me can see that." She was right, of course. She wasn't encouraged at home or at school to take her mind seriously, whereas people all over the place were taking her body seriously.

Jayne went to college because Paul was going, because eminently middle-class Vera and Harry expected it and because, like marriage, it was glamorous. During a period when girls were going to college to find husbands, Jayne wasn't heavily taxed. Charlsa thinks Jayne also wanted to go to Austin because its drama school was particularly good. Its graduates from that period include Rip Torn (who married Ann Wedgeworth), Tom Jones and Harvey Schmidt, the authors of *The Fantasticks,* and Pat Hingle.

The University of Texas was in a state of transition, having just admitted its first black students. The student body was far more active in fraternity exploits than politics. Students squeezed themselves into phone booths and raided panties.

Women in college in 1950 divided into two camps according to the timeless adage: Good girls go home and go to bed; nice girls go to bed and go home. College men found sex in short supply. There weren't enough nice girls to go around, and nobody really wanted a girl who'd been around anyway. Men made every effort to seduce the good girls. If, however, the seduction succeeded, the good girl became, of course, merely nice. The good girl had to confront the dilemma of maintaining a virtuous exterior and a sexy demeanor. The good girl knew that her reputation hung on her ability to welch prettily on the evening's debt. She had to cling to her virginity, indicating all the while that she might be willing to give it up. The product of this tension was the technical virgin. In the face of male frustration and disappointment, the good girl had to have the confidence that her date was secretly glad she had resisted, pleased that she was still good and that he was off

○ ○ ○ ○ ○ ○ ○ ○ ○ ○ ○ ○ ○ ○ ○ ○ ○ ○ ○ ○ ○ ○ ○ ○ ○ ○ ○ ○ ○ ○ ○ ○ ○ ○ ○ ○ ○ ○ ○

the hook. Nice girls worried less about their reputations than their date's blue balls or the accusation of cock-teasing. Good girls knew better. They understood the implicit ambivalence about sex and knew their lot was to be chased and chaste. They understood that men were obliged to try to score but that they would willingly settle for third base. The good girl never forgot the difference between the Phi Gam Sweetheart and the Psi U Mattress.

Consider the institution of the pantie raid. A bunch of young men invaded a girls' dorm and captured the pantie trophy. The spoils were a sex symbol, but decidedly not sex. The activity occasioned much merriment, blue jokes, giggling and feigned embarrassment on the part of the girls and was, in toto, absolutely asexual. It seems foreign and almost sad today. Behind the snickers and wisecracks are echoes of fear and a sort of innocence. The raid was like a rite at the profane monument of sex. Stealing drawers became sexual conquest for the boys and a token defloration without consequences for the girls. Streaking is another asexual act, but it's beyond sex and into Dada. Pantie raiding was a presexual fumble, while streaking is an effort to revive some interest in nudity by placing it in incongruous contexts.

Later, on stage, Jayne brilliantly manipulated America's peculiar love-hate relationship with sex. She became an artist at stimulating sexual interest without demanding anything. Her message was the subtle and reassuring Look, but You Don't Have to Touch. She always kept in mind what men wanted women to be and the fearsome side of sex. She came to symbolize the cheerful, easy lay, whom one didn't have to lay at all.

As a married student and mother, Jayne missed out on some basics of college life. She never lived in a dormitory or a sorority. She didn't go out on dates and spend the evening necking to Frank Sinatra. Charlsa remembers how

○ ○ ○ ○ ○ ○ ○ ○ ○ ○ ○ ○ ○ ○ ○ ○ ○ ○ ○ ○ ○ ○ ○ ○ ○ ○ ○ ○ ○ ○ ○ ○ ○ ○ ○ ○ ○ ○ ○ ○ ○ ○

hard it was on Jayne who wanted so much to be a regular college girl.

"Gosh, she was sort of stranded because she couldn't get away from the house. I remember she wanted to take classes and she wanted to be one of the schoolgirls, but she never really had the experience of being in college. It was really a trying thing, here she was seventeen years old and saddled with all this responsibility. I remember for a semester she was sort of at odds because she couldn't get with it. She wanted to be a student and yet nobody would accept her.

"Boy, when she was walking down the street, then people started noticing her. She was pushing Jayne Marie in a baby carriage and two guys stopped in a car. They pulled over to the side and said, 'Hey, how are you?' And she said, 'Oh, fine.' They said, 'What have you got in the baby carriage?' 'A baby.' They both got out to look because they couldn't believe it. They said, 'Is it yours?' She said, 'Yeah, it's mine.' They didn't stop to talk. They just drove off. She would turn heads. She kind of came into her own when she got to college, which was kind of sad because it was too late because she had all that responsibility."

The "own" Jayne came into was her body. She had enormous breasts, made to seem even more enormous because they rested on a wide ribcage. She learned through ogling, whistling and leering that her body could provide her with attention. The size of those breasts, important as they seemed to every man she met, became crucial to her. She came to see herself as others saw her. Her mystique grew to recapitulate her physique. She was trapped in an overblown, phantasmagoric piece of flesh, and what could she do but take it seriously. Her body and the reaction it inspired determined her course of action. Her build never allowed her room to reflect on what she wanted, since what she was was what all men seemed to want. An accommodating woman, she wanted to give it to them. A plain, flat-chested Jayne might have chosen to be a teacher, a veterinarian, a farmer's wife, a chemical engineer. But Jayne, hungry as she was for approval, surveyed her assets and found the most valuable one to be her forty-inch bust. Society told her she was desirable beyond the ordinary. So she dressed in tight clothes, created a commotion, and developed in the direction in which she was having the most success.

As Ann said when she encountered Jayne after a year in Austin, "You've really changed." Jayne said, "I used to be afraid. I'm not afraid anymore."

Jayne and Paul rented a small campus apartment in Austin. "Really tacky," said Charlsa. They had two rooms, a lamp and a chair for which they competed. When Paul won the chair, Jayne sat on his lap.

Jayne, the cook, made "real good fudge. She was not, to be frank, what you call a homemaker. You know her mother would shoo her out of the kitchen. She'd say, 'Get out, you're making me nervous.' Then she was thrown into the situation of having to cook. They ate a lot of hamburgers. Out.

"Every time they wanted a good meal, they'd go down to the place called Somewhere, where you got a Someburger. You had to have a hundred Someburgers and then you became a native Austinite; everybody was always working on their Someburgers."

On February 20, 1951, when Jayne had been in Austin a couple of months, she wrote her parents a breathless letter.

Dearest Mamma and Daddy,

Here it is midnight — my first free moment, believe me! I have so many things to say and to thank you for that I hardly know quite where to begin!

o o o o o o o o o o o o o o o o o o o o o o o o o o o o o o o o o o o o o o o o

First (as I take things as I think of them) I loved the cute little Valentine you sent me with that dollar bill in it, and thank you *so, so* much!  We're saving that for Carnation milk probably!  And I certainly felt wonderful all over when I got those *beautiful* Valentines from you, Mamma, and you Daddy.  It made me feel all "fluttery" too.  And little Jayne Marie's cat was luscious!  Thank you — thank you!  I'll keep it for her and when she gets to be a big girl I'll show it to her.  No kidding, Mamma, when it came I held it in front of her for about five minutes while she was sitting on my lap, and her little mouth dropped open — she looked and looked at it then I told her it was from "her Grammy that loves her" and she burst right into a smile!  I certainly thank you both for that last dollar, too, it was precious of youall to be so sweet!  And, Daddy, your letter was so darling, too, and thank you!

. . . We took Jayne Marie to the doctor and he said she has gained wonderfully — the maximum amount she could possibly gain, too.  She's on cereals, vegetables, and fruit, and her little cheeks are pink!  She weighs 13 lbs. 13 ozs. and everywhere we take her they say what a little butterball she is!  Never have I seen such a happy one either.  Her hair is auburn now, but her eyes are still as blue as a summer sky!  She is always ga-ga-ga-ing.

I guess Paul's mamma has asked you to send me down my green filmy strapless formal — with stole for me!  The dance is this Saturday night, and it's quite an important one!  Certainly thank you!

It is one o'clock now, and I have to be in school by nine in the morning so I'd better blow youall a goodnight kiss!  You're the dearest folks in the world to me, and never forget it!

ALL MY LOVE

JAYNE

Jayne's handwriting was big and dramatic.  Before she started dotting her i's with hearts, she used circles, dear to the hearts of all American high school girls.  Her backhand signature dripped baroque decorations. The letter is thoroughly Jayne, an excess of goo and exclamation points.

She was always lavish in her gratitude. She devoted an abundant amount of space thanking Harry and Vera for what seems like a pretty modest contribution to the Mansfield cash resources. But Jayne was genuinely pleased and grateful when anyone did anything for her. She later wrote thank-you notes to every columnist who mentioned her in the papers.

After floundering around for a bit, Jayne enrolled in some courses in the drama department. It wasn't very exciting since university policy was to give the choice parts to the seniors, leaving the freshmen to paint the sets.

Jayne organized a day-care arrangement to suit her schedule. Charlsa says, "She would appear on campus with the baby carriage and sit until Paul would get out of class; he would then go sit with the baby carriage for an hour so she could go to class. She became a campus figure at that time because nobody had babies."

Jayne remained very close to the Peerses during her year in Austin. Vera recalled one weekend in November when the young couple came up for a football game. "They were supposed to leave at a certain time and they didn't leave, and we drove them down." Harry elaborates, "We left here about one o'clock, got down there about five. And we left about five-thirty, turned around and came home." Vera says, "We had to. Harry had to be in the office that morning. And it was Jaynie Marie's first birthday. Jaynie was just as happy as could be and she and Paul were playing games in the back seat of the car and she would laugh and say, 'Well, don't bother Mama about that because Mama doesn't like to play those games.' And I said, 'No, I've got all I can do here with Jaynie Marie.' She was on my lap. That was a wild ride. You have no idea of the stuff we've been through."

Vera remembers Jayne saying laughingly that "she was going to get married, have her babies, give them to me to take care of and go to college. I thought, oh, that would be just fine. I just laughed it off. I never took a statement like that seriously. Well, she almost did that."

Jayne Marie delighted her mother, but Jayne was seventeen and had other things to do. Instead of following Vera's example of devoted motherhood, she put the exemplar to work for her. She let Vera pick up with Jaynie Marie where she'd left off with Jayne so Vera had another creature to baby. By giving Vera some responsibility for Jayne Marie, Jayne was giving her baby-loving mother much joy. In a way it was one of Jayne's attempts to placate her mother. The baby distracted Vera from Jayne, occupied her and acted as a buffer between them. Ironically, Jayne was also bringing herself closer to her mother. Raising Jayne Marie brought mother and daughter together in a new pursuit and a new tense intimacy.

Early in 1952, Paul Mansfield was drafted. MacArthur had been recalled from Korea in the spring of 1951. The Communists had pushed UN troops back, and they were slowly advancing toward the 38th Parallel again. MacArthur was calling for aid to Chiang Kai-shek and United States bombing north of the Yalu River to break the stalemate. Truman was opposed. The nation was confused about the reasons for the war, certain only that thousands of Americans were dying in what seemed an endless and hopeless fight for a dubious government.

Before being shipped overseas, Paul did a short stint at Camp Gordon in Georgia. Jayne accompanied him and amused herself by practicing in a leotard what she referred to as ballet in full view of the drill field. She also made regular appearances at the base swimming pool in noteworthy outfits, including a velvet bikini. She undoubtedly

o o o o o o o o o o o o o o o o o o o o o o o o o o o o o o o o o o o o

alleviated whatever boredom the camp was suffering from. She said later, "It's a good thing I wasn't an enemy agent. I could have turned Camp Gordon into a ghost town if I'd accepted all the kind invitations extended to me."

Jayne was having some theatrical success at Camp Gordon. She and Charlsa exchanged letters. "I remember writing to Jayne and saying, have you seen that new girl, Marilyn Monroe? You look just like her. I got back a letter saying 'the only resemblance between me and Marilyn Monroe is that we've both got two eyes, two ears and a body.' But I think other people told her this. She really looked great and she kept her weight down. I think she got every part she wanted. She said she was the lead in this show and the lead in that show. I can just imagine these army guys going mad over her at the base and her deciding that she was a great actress."

Before Paul was shipped overseas he and Jayne concluded a treaty providing that they would all go to Hollywood when Paul got out of the service and Jayne would try to get into the movies. If, after six months she wasn't successful, she agreed to return to Dallas.

It may have been a relief to both Mansfields when Paul was shipped to Korea. He was not happy with her exhibitionism and her growing determination to be an actress. And she was not very happy with him. Jayne had been crazy about the Paul of her imagination, the Older Man, the Quartet Singer, the College Man. She liked his looks and his experience and his observance of extravagant courtship rituals. The external Paul looked pretty good. She didn't worry much about their attitudes toward work, money, success, style and love. She was more interested in seeing herself and Paul. What a good-looking couple, people would say, and how happy they must be. Isn't he lucky to have such a beautiful wife, and isn't she

o o o o o o o o o o o o o o o o o o o o o o o o o o o o o o o o o o o o o o o

lucky . . . But, after a time, she wasn't feeling lucky at all. She was depressed by the dullness of their lives, by Paul's lack of ambition, and was caught up in her own desperation to do better.

They were very different. She was flamboyant and he was conservative. Harry recognized that "they had different ambitions and goals. Some people have a lot of push. Some don't. Paul had none. He tended to drift. Whatever was done was done because of Jaynie's push."

Vera concluded, "Paul didn't do very much toward that marriage. Jaynie gave more to that marriage than Paul did. He just never wanted her to get into the movies."

Jayne returned from Dallas and enrolled at SMU. She took courses in drama, abnormal psychology (which may be why Mickey Hargitay once said of her, "In school Jayne minored in psychiatry") and biology ("I'll never forget those horrible frogs I used to cut up in biology lab").

Ann Wedgeworth, who was studying drama at SMU, ran into Jayne. Ann recalled that Jayne had died her hair black. "It looked great on her," Ann went on. "She had always wanted to be a movie star. But then she had a lot more confidence in herself. She had really gotten into the idea of going out to Hollywood."

When Jayne came back Paul insisted that she get her own apartment. He didn't want her living at home. Charlsa thought it was "absurd," but Paul wanted to set up his own life separate from the Peerses. He sensed Jayne's intense attachment to Vera and wanted to disengage mother and daughter. Jayne was living more comfortably now that she had Paul's army allotment and she could afford a small modern apartment near SMU. Nevertheless she spent a great deal of time at the Peerses' popping in and out regularly.

In 1952, Baruch Lumet, Sidney's father, came to Dallas

and set up the Dallas Institute of the Performing Arts. Jayne came to him through an editor on the Dallas *Morning News*. Lumet said, "She studied with me for several months privately. She later stopped taking lessons. She could not afford paying me and paying a baby sitter. My wife and I decided to take care of the little girl and make it possible for her to continue studying. After a year or so I took her into the first stage production of *Death of a Salesman*."

Jayne also got a couple of parts in plays on a local television station. And she became Miss Photoflash, 1952, beginning what was to be a long and singular list of beauty awards.

In the years since 1950, Jayne had changed and matured somewhat. Charlsa had dinner with her one night in Dallas, and they started talking about their high school lunch companion who had married the SMU freshman. "I remember her saying that she'd seen this girl. She'd been married five or six years and she had a couple of children. She was very dowdy and middle-aged-looking and wasn't even twenty-one. Jaynie thought that was so sad. I think her ideas had changed radically." The glamor of marriage had all but disappeared for Jayne. Not that she wasn't to try it again. But she had been putting her own life in perspective and had got along quite well without Paul.

Armistice negotiations began with Korea on April 27, 1953, but it was a full year before Paul Mansfield came home. Jayne had hardly let him in the house before they were off and running to California. Paul was disinclined to honor his part of the going-to-Hollywood bargain, but one of Jayne's characteristics was tremendous persistence and she got her way.

Before Jayne left she and Lumet worked up a scene from *Joan of Arc* in case she were to get a screen test. "This was the first time I made her cry with bitter tears. She was happy," remembered Lumet. Paul and Jayne came to say goodby and after they left Lumet called his friend Milton Lewis at Paramount to notify him that talent was on its way.

It was a sad day for Vera. "They came up and spent the night with us. And, *oh,* how *well* I remember that morning. I thought well, I didn't want to see her go and I was almost breaking my heart and I thought well, I'll send them off nice. And I don't know how many chickens I fried and I baked a chocolate cake and made a potato salad. I don't know how I did it, but I did it that morning. And so they went off loaded down with everything in Jaynie's red Buick.

"They just decided to go because she wanted to go. She was going to go out and be a movie star. That was it. She just announced it. I said, 'Well, how are you going to do that?' 'Well,' she said, 'I'm going to do it,' and that was all."

Jayne had accumulated a number of animals in Paul's absence, so the couple drove off with three dogs, three cats, two birds, a white rabbit and a gila monster. Paul was not fond of animals. The pets were in a trailer hooked onto the car and referred to as "Noah's Ark."

Jayne's fondness for animals became a trademark. Charlsa said, "She adored animals. She always had a dog and took it around with her every place. It wasn't to attract attention, but I think in a demanding situation it was like a security blanket, having that little dog that completely loved her. They were little tiny, bitty Chihuahuas and she could just tuck them in her arms." Jayne, when questioned about her menagerie, said, "When someone wants to give me something, I ask for an animal. I love pets, and besides, it makes good copy."

o o o o o o o o o o o o o o o o o o o o o o o o o o o o o o o o o o o o o

Equally good copy was Jayne's later description of crossing the California border.  She claimed to have gotten out of the car, knelt and kissed the ground.  "I am home," she said and started to weep.

# Dumb Blonde

"Well, I try to be dumb."
*Martha Mitchell, April 1974*

HOLLYWOOD WOMEN in 1954 were sexy and stupid or funny and stupid. They were encouraged not to try to be both since sex or the woman would suffer. If a sexy woman got too funny she became threatening. Similarly, a funny woman couldn't be too smart or she became overwhelming. Rita Hayworth, Susan Hayward, Joanne Dru, Jane Russell, Kim Novak — they were all serious.

Lucille Ball, Eve Arden, Martha Raye, Gale Storm, Gracie Allen, Ann Sothern, Imogene Coca — they were all sexless. Lucille Ball yelled and connived with Vivian Vance. Eve Arden pined ridiculously for limp Mr. Boynton. Martha Raye turned her face into silly putty. Gale Storm gargled and rolled her eyes as Charlie Farrell's "Little Margie." George Burns straightened dizzy Gracie out. Ann Sothern had a typewriter instead of a man. And Imogen Coca played Sid Caesar's incompetent wife who wrecked the family car and was afraid to tell.

Jayne wanted to find a place for herself among these women. Because of her sexuality she had to steer away from the humor which came naturally to her. But in time she came to challenge the barrier between sex and comedy.

Jayne and Paul found themselves a small apartment in Los Angeles at Fulton and Van Nuys. Paul had trouble getting a job but eventually went to work for a roofing company. Jayne took a series of badly paying jobs, selling popcorn at the Stanley Warner Theatre, checking hats, teaching dance.

The very first thing Jayne did in Los Angeles was to call Paramount. As her story went, she got Milton Lewis's secretary on the phone and said, "My name's Jayne Mansfield and I want to be a star. I just arrived from Dallas where I won a beauty contest."

The secretary is said to have replied that Paramount already had a star, but she set up an appointment for Jayne with Mr. Lewis because of Lumet's forewarning. Jayne made the test she and Lumet had worked up, wearing a strapless top and a red flaring skirt. Lewis was kind to her, suggested that she lose some weight but didn't give her a contract. Jayne said later, "Somehow, I've always suspected it was something to do with the skirt."

Partially rebuffed, Jayne went out and got herself an agent, Robert Schwartz, whose contribution to her career was to have her bleach her hair. With her new platinum hair she had become the complete cliché. Peroxided hair gave off stupid signals as efficiently as a sign saying "I am a nincompoop." After that she stood herself to another screen test, this time *The Seven Year Itch* at Warner Brothers. Mervin LeRoy liked what he saw, but nothing happened.

Jayne was fairly desperate. She and Paul were fighting. Paul was anxious to return to Dallas, settle down and forget Jayne's Hollywood nonsense. After three months in Los Angeles, he wanted to renege on his bargain. Jayne was determined to stick it out until she landed some kind of part.

She was twenty-one and came into $5000 from her Grandmother Palmer's estate, a trust fund set up in 1945 totaling $36,340.  With her first money Jayne made a $4000 down payment on an $18,000 house on Wanda Park Drive in Beverly Hills.  It is surrounded by trees and bougainvillea and seems to grow out of the hillside.  Up behind the house is a patio and a small swimming pool which Jayne had put in later.

Paul and she were getting along very badly and by October of that year Paul had moved out and back to Dallas. Jayne's six months were up, but she never really meant to leave at all.

The same month that Paul left she got a bit part in a "Lux Video Theater" television play called *"The Angel Went AWOL."*  "I was paid three hundred dollars for sitting at a piano and speaking ten lines of dialogue."  The next month she got to play a nymphomaniac for $150 in a rare movie called *The Female Jungle* with Lawrence Tierney and John Carradine.  Jayne said, *"Hangover* [later called *The Female Jungle]* was finished in two weeks and led to nothing."

Just before Christmas Jayne met a young man who was to help her get some of the things she wanted.  Jim Byron, currently proprietor of an agency called Destiny, Inc., has the deep, rich voice of a radio announcer.  He has a pale face, reddish brown hair with some gray and wears wire spectacles.  He won't tell his age and looks anywhere from twenty-eight to fifty-eight depending on the light and what he's saying.  He has a glib manner, marred by the odd malapropism.  There is an unsettling Dorian Gray quality about Byron, some trace of corruption in his face.  He currently manages Yvette Mimieux and seems to be on hard times.  He drives a new Eldorado which he bought, he says, to get good service from parking attendants at restaurants and bars.  He is not a check grabber.

He is reluctant to talk about Jayne and makes a speech about how history doesn't interest him. He is only happy in the present thinking about the future. He emphasizes that he likes to think positively about people and things. He doesn't like knocking people, although he is not a consistent booster when it comes to some of Jayne's intimates.

A friend of Jim's brought Jayne to his office in December of 1954. Jayne was wearing a very tight green cotton knit dress. When Jim saw her he immediately had a vision of Jayne delivering his Christmas Scotch to reporters. He got her a snug red dress for a sexy female Santa Claus and a sack of bottles. She went to the press room which the Los Angeles *Mirror* and the *Times* shared. She walked through the room and, as Byron remembers, "The linotypers were dropping their type and she was digging it up." She handed each reporter a bottle of whiskey, leaned over, whispered "Merry Christmas" and kissed him on the back of the neck. She was a sensation. She moved to the *Herald-Examiner* and repeated the performance. The next day her picture was in the papers, one of the best Christmas presents she ever had.

Jim was a hotshot young press agent when he met Jayne. He was responsible for getting Marilyn Maxwell photographed with a leopard in her swimming pool. He used to take a Magic Slate into the shower with him to jot down publicity stunts.

Byron and his attitude about publicity is one of the keys to Jayne's career. Byron says of that period in his life, "I was looking for a chick to prove that I was the world's greatest living press agent." Jayne and Jim had perfectly meeting wishes. She wanted to start her career moving and felt that publicity was the best way. Publicity had indeed been at its best throughout the last twenty years in Hollywood. As the fifties drew to a close this was no longer true. Studios were no longer prepared to do mas-

sive publicity and stars began to find it chic to hide. Jayne
and Jim came together in the last days of the publicity
stunt and they both took a kind of uninhibited, adolescent
pleasure in concocting bigger and better schemes. As another publicist pointed out later, neither of them had any
taste so the escapades were either delightful or excrucia-
ting, depending on luck.

Jim was the first professional Jayne had met who was
seriously interested in her career and who could do something for her. He was as enthusiastic about her as she
was, and for the same reason. His career could be made to
the extent that hers could.

Jayne's Santa Claus imitation was the beginning of a
long and cordial friendship between her and the press.
She was always nice to reporters — as Jim says, "A very up
human being. She was fun and she was copy. She never
refused the press. In a period when it was the thing to
hide, you could call her up at four A.M. and she would give
you a story."

Jayne studied hard with Jim about how to handle newsmen. He told her, for example, that columnist Harrison
Carroll had a certain weakness for disease and pain anec-
dotes. At a party that night Jim overheard Jayne saying to
Carroll, "I had this terrible accident and my ankle . . ."
"She picked up instantly," says Jim. "She became in time
the world's greatest press agent. I think I overdid it. I
made her believe that publicity was the greatest God."

Vera and Harry Peers drove out to Beverly Hills for
Christmas that year. Jaynie Marie was just four, old
enough to appreciate the lavishness of her mother and
grandmother. She collected a formidable pile of presents,
clothes, dolls, stuffed animals and toys. Mrs. Peers remembers that as an especially happy Christmas. "Jaynie
was very loving and happy. She had gleaming eyes. You
were never lonely when she was there."

In January Byron wangled Jayne a ticket on a plane that was flying to Silver Springs, Florida. Howard Hughes had chartered the plane to transport press and dignitaries to the premiere of Jane Russell's new movie, *Underwater*. The film was to be shown to a submerged audience clad in bathing suits and Aqua-Lungs. At the last minute Jayne got on board and managed to sit next to Joseph Schoenfeld, then editor of *Daily Variety*. Schoenfeld and Jayne hit it off, and he was responsible for filing the first big stories about her in the most important trade journal in the industry.

The high point of the Florida trip was the pool party. Jayne showed up early in a bikini that was as astonishing as it was flimsy. The photographers had used up all their film by the time Jane Russell, Debbie Reynolds and the other guests appeared. Meanwhile, in keeping with subsequent mishaps, Jayne's bathing suit had come undone in the water and the press was goggle-eyed watching her reclaim her bra. All in all it was an unprecedented success for Jayne and Byron.

"*Underwater* made Jayne news," recalls Byron. "Hughes sent word that he wanted her under contract for one thousand dollars a week. At the time he had forty or fifty girls under contract, and they were all hidden away."

On her return, Byron introduced Jayne to an independent agent, Bill Shiffrin. Shriffrin is a short, feisty, self-made man in his sixties with deep sunken eyes and firm convictions about everything. He is vigorous and honest and doesn't suffer fools. Shiffrin and his beautiful young wife, Grace, live across from Liberace in a modern house composed of several A-frames with a breathtaking view of Los Angeles. They are devoted to each other and have the engaging habit of necking while giving an interview.

Shiffrin remembers his first meeting with Jayne. "When I first saw her I honestly thought I saw two miniature dirigibles followed by a gorgeous blonde in a golden dress. Can you imagine? A table for three and two dirigibles."

Bill said, "We need a new glamor girl."

Jayne said, "That's me."

She convinced Bill who says, "The reason I started her was that we had a Novak and a Monroe and I thought the town could use another blonde."

After her successes as Miss Photoflash 1952 and Miss Third Platoon 1952, Jayne and Jim got busy on other titles. She became Miss Queen of the Chihuahua Show, Miss Orchid, Miss Nylon (sweaters), Miss 100% Pure (syrup), Miss One for the Road (coffee), Best Dressed Woman of the Theater, Miss Negligee (the sponsors: "Miss Mansfield is the most interesting person who depicts what negligees are for"), Miss Blue Bonnet of Austin, Texas, Miss Texas Tomato, Miss Electric Switch, Miss Cotton Queen, Miss Freeway, Miss July Fourth, Miss Standard Foods, Miss Four Alarm, Gas Station Queen. "I think the only thing I ever turned down was a chance to be Miss Roquefort Cheese because it didn't sound right," she remarked.

Meanwhile, negotiations among Shiffrin and several studios were going on to determine who would sign Jayne. Shiffrin told Warner's Hal Wallis about Jayne. "The next day," Bill says, "they made her an offer without talking to me. Byron tried to convince her to take a lousy contract. Meanwhile Darryl Zanuck at Twentieth-Century Fox was waiting to see her old screen test of *The Seven Year Itch*."

Byron picks up the story. "Jayne wanted to take Wallis' offer of one hundred fifty dollars a week. If she didn't take it Wallis was threatening to bar her from Warner Brothers. At the same time Walter Kane was calling every day for Howard Hughes. Shiffrin was threatening me and Kane was threatening me and Wallis was going to have me thrown off the lot."

Shiffrin had the screen test "frozen until Warners gave

○ ○ ○ ○ ○ ○ ○ ○ ○ ○ ○ ○ ○ ○ ○ ○ ○ ○ ○ ○ ○ ○ ○ ○ ○ ○ ○ ○ ○ ○ ○ ○ ○ ○ ○ ○ ○

me an answer. Wallis gave me an ultimatum. I advised
Jayne not to take it. The money was lousy and the deal
was bad. I told Byron that she could really make it big, but
finally she took two hundred and fifty dollars a week to
start at Warner Brothers with a six-month contract with op-
tions."

Byron introduced Jayne to Gregson Bautzer, a legendary
Hollywood lawyer. He represents a great many sectors of
the movie industry, studios, performers, directors, pro-
ducers and so on. In addition to his clientele, Bautzer is
famous for having squired around more starlets than any
living roue. Today Bautzer has white hair, hip glasses and
terrific teeth. He has a lecherous sort of wit and quotes
George Jessel regularly ("Behind every beautiful woman,
there's a beautiful behind," etc.) He drives a silver Rolls
and spends a lot of time in the Polo Lounge of the Beverly
Hills Hotel where the ex-Philip Morris page ("Call for
Philip Morris") brings him phones.

Jayne said of Bautzer, "He is like a regular standby.
Always there to take a girl out on the most elegant parties.
Even though he dates the most famous women in the
world, he makes a girl feel like she is the only one. He is
extremely attentive. Greg will dash across the room just to
light a girl's cigarette."

A girl might not be flattered to find that Bautzer denies
ever having any but a business relationship with her. "I
liked her because she was flat-assed out honest. We remained good friends. She was an honest dame and I say
that in the affectionate sense. I found her simpatico. She
was so vulnerable and terribly insecure. There was something overblown about her figure, something not sexy but
pathetic. I would rather have gone to bed with Agnes
Moorehead."

Whatever the particulars of Jayne's relation with Bautzer,
in general she made no distinction between her business

o o o o o o o o o o o o o o o o o o o o o o o o o o o o o o o o o o o o o o o o o o

and social lives, or rather her business was her social life. As Byron says, "She lived her career twenty-four hours a day."

Shiffrin remembers this same confusion. A year later he was "standing by her pink Jag and she said, 'You and I could be Melcher and Doris Day.' I said, 'I'm not Melcher. I'm Bill Shiffrin and I've got a wife and three kids.' "

Jayne never really had a love affair without first consulting her career. It wasn't all that deliberate, but she was so single-minded that all the important men in her life were involved intimately with her profession. Her two subsequent husbands both acted as managers and business advisers, and her last lover, a lawyer, was indispensable to her in sorting out the legal entanglements in which she found herself. Jayne was the common interest between her men and herself. She was interested in her career, and they were too, sometimes for their own advancement. Sometimes, because Jayne's body was her career, it was hard to know who had whose best interest at whose heart.

Shiffrin feels that she never understood that sex and business were separate. When one of her advisers did something successful for her she would often offer sex as a reward. She and Byron had a halfhearted sort of affair for the first six months they worked together. He describes that period as one of "gigantic closeness and romance. Whoever was around was the total focal point of her interest. She made you feel that you were so important."

Jayne was making no money so she arranged to give 10 percent of her future earnings to Byron, 10 percent to Shiffrin and 5 percent to Bautzer. Bautzer says, "I don't think I ever charged her a fee."

Jayne and Jim were elaborating Jayne's dream of becoming a star. "Ever since I was a little girl I was convinced I was going to be a big star someday. I haven't got there yet, but I will. It's eighty percent determination and

○ ○ ○ ○ ○ ○ ○ ○ ○ ○ ○ ○ ○ ○ ○ ○ ○ ○ ○ ○ ○ ○ ○ ○ ○ ○ ○ ○ ○ ○ ○ ○ ○ ○ ○

twenty percent talent. I know I'll make it. I'm the girl with the built-in drive."

She and Byron put together a style Jayne would substitute for substance. In the early days, the quality of style didn't matter very much. Byron feels that "She was the satire of all dumb blondes. Shiffrin and Bautzer tried to do something wrong. They kept trying to make her conservative. Eventually she would have graduated from the sexpot stuff and would have evolved with public approval after establishing their affection. You can't be highly selective or you end up by doing nothing. She made bomb after bomb, but the guy in Iowa still loved the pictures even if they were bad. Jayne had an image and we had to capitalize on that and push forward. In the beginning you can only make the product famous, not necessarily acceptable. You have to think day to day on the spur of the moment. One time Jayne arrived and I posed her by a sign on a crane which was there. The sign said, 'Excess Frontage Overhang.' It wasn't a problem coming up with individual stunts for her."

Byron's critics feel that he didn't help Jayne's career, but in the beginning it wasn't clear. Jayne thoroughly approved of Jim's approach, found that not only did it get results but also it was fun. She was naturally uninhibited and the stunts pleased the exhibitionist and prankster in her. Byron says, "You have to have a gimmick." It was true that without a gimmick Jayne was just another busty girl who wanted to break into the movies.

She said later, "Well, I feel that any girl who has an, uh, unusual figure is really under a handicap. Oh, I used my figure to get into this business. Almost any studio will hire you just for shots and publicity and scenery."

She had no interest in hanging around as scenery. She wanted "To feel satisfied with myself. To know that I have arrived. To be a good actress. To be liked. To be a big personality. The real stars are not actors or actresses. They're personalities. The quality of making everyone stop in their tracks is what I work at."

Back to the chase for the elusive personality. The professional personality is human form without content. The only thing that can be said for sure about it is that it appears on TV talk shows. Personalities don't do, they are. Jayne bought Byron's concept of satirizing all dumb blondes. While that seems like a passive state, it requires great skill and exhausting activity to achieve. The personality must be seen to exist. It has no meaning without a public. The condition is not restful or secure. Many of Jayne's troubles stemmed from that fact. An actress can know that she has performed well or badly. A surgeon has evidence that he is a good or a bad surgeon. But a personality, because she is nothing but an assortment of traits, can never rest easy in the knowledge that she is a good personality. Someone might not like her.

The issue was more complicated than it had been in high school, where having personality meant only one thing. Modifying the quality with "good" or "great" was redundant since there was only one kind, and Jayne didn't have it. As a performer, Jayne could incorporate sex into her personality. "Dumb blonde" was a legitimate expression of one kind of American woman. Of course, just as playing up sex was a second-rate route to popularity in high school, so in Hollywood it was classier to be Audrey Hepburn than Jayne Mansfield.

To the extent that Hollywood could use what Byron so accurately and poignantly called "a satire of all dumb blondes who ever lived," the country betrayed its brutalized sexual attitudes. The laughs Jayne got ridiculed her sexuality. No one could look at her without thinking of sex, and the laughter wasn't because sex is funny, but that

o o o o o o o o o o o o o o o o o o o o o o o o o o o o o o o o o o

it and she were obscene and grotesque, desirable but
disgusting, a necessary evil like prostitution. She inspired
lust, revulsion and mockery. She provoked the crudest
kind of fantasies and then had to take the blame for them
although they weren't hers. But she'd been cast by her
breasts, costumed in her bleached hair and directed by
Byron and the prevailing sexual winds.

During the months Jayne was under contract to Warner
Brothers she got parts in a couple of dismal films including
*Pete Kelly's Blues* with Jack Webb and *Illegal* with Edward
G. Robinson. She also made a picture called *Hell on Frisco
Bay*.

Shiffrin says, "She wore out her welcome at Warner
Brothers. I told her to be a little aloof, not such an eager
beaver. But she wouldn't listen. She came to me and right
away she was an executive. She thought she knew it all.
She had to steal every space in town every day."

Bautzer has some of the same complaints about Jayne.
"She had the chance to be successful and it was her own
mistake that she wasn't. She got involved later with too
many people, four lawyers, four agents. You can only
operate with one trusted adviser. She got involved with
the wrong people both in an advisory capacity and in a
lover capacity."

And Byron chimes in, "Jayne began listening to too
many people. Jayne wanted to hear what she wanted to
hear."

A case in point is the Mansfield hot-water bottle. Byron
thinks that one of his greatest publicity ideas was making
small inflatable Jayne Mansfield hot-water bottles and fill-
ing a swimming pool with them. A company sold them
and Jayne got the royalties. He wanted to go on and make
a life-size Mansfield rubber float. Bautzer and Shiffrin
thought both ideas vulgar.

○ ○ ○ ○ ○ ○ ○ ○ ○ ○ ○ ○ ○ ○ ○ ○ ○ ○ ○ ○ ○ ○ ○ ○ ○ ○ ○ ○ ○ ○ ○ ○ ○ ○ ○ ○

Bill says, "She got involved with the rotgut of Hollywood and they made those Mansfield rubber dolls. She went through the whole gamut of Hollywood nonsense."

Each of Jayne's advisers is right in his way. The thing that Shiffrin and Bautzer worried about happened. As Shiffrin puts it, "She became a freak." But she loved doing it. She loved all kinds of attention, she loved making a spectacle of herself. It was fun. She was out for a good time. And Byron, because he wasn't critical and because he loved the outrageous as much as Jayne, became her closest ally in the sleazy, cheesecake promotion campaign that became her career. She started out opening supermarkets and she opened them for the rest of her life. At the very peak of her fame she would dash off to cut a ribbon at a new bowling alley or officiate at the grand première of a Kentucky Fried Chicken franchise. The patterns she and Jim established right in the beginning persisted long after Jayne and Jim had parted company. Eventually Jayne became the gimmick. But in the beginning, they thought up new gimmicks every day. Jayne would go into a drugstore and buy a pair of falsies. "That was to show I have a sense of humor," she explained.

Meanwhile, Bill Shiffrin was busy making the deal which would make Jayne famous virtually overnight. "Five or six months into the Warner Brothers contract, Dana Andrews gave me the script of *Will Success Spoil Rock Hunter?* Marilyn Maxwell had turned the part down. I didn't think much of the script.

"At the same time, Paul Wendkos, a director, wanted my client Dan Duryea for a part in *The Burglar* to be shot in Philadelphia. There was also a part in the movie for a bombshell. I took Wendkos to Warners to show him the test Jayne did of *The Seven Year Itch*. Paul was very negative. 'She's just for truck drivers to drool over. She's too cheap looking.'

o o o o o o o o o o o o o o o o o o o o o o o o o o o o o o o o o

"In the middle of the screening I got a huge idea. I stood up and started waving my arms around, yelling, 'I'm going to make a star out of this broad.' I had suddenly remembered *Rock Hunter*. I told Paul, 'She's too good for you, she's for me and this play.' "

Bill called Marty Baum, his New York representative, told him about the play and said, "Unless you've got Monroe, I've got the only girl who can do it. She's got every qualification for the part. She's the most uninhibited dame I ever met." Bill sent Jayne's picture to Baum and George Axelrod, who had written the play and was going to direct it. Baum called back hysterical. "Can she talk? She's got it."

Bill then told Jayne that she was going to New York to read for a play. "A what?" she said. "I only want movies."

"It'll only save us five years making you a star," said Shiffrin. "I bought her a ticket and air-mailed her to New York. On that same day Wendkos called and said, 'I'll buy her for *The Burglar*.' Baum had to get her a baby sitter since she dragged Jayne Marie around with her everywhere. She read and got the part."

Bill then had to renegotiate Jayne out of her Warner Brothers commitment. Jayne wanted to remain in the contract. As Bill said, "She liked the *insecurity* of a term contract." Bill proposed that Warners lend her to Wendkos for $5000 or $10,000. He added that she would be doing a play and would return to Warners a hot star. Then Warners could pick up her option at $300 or so afterward. Warners chose to drop her.

Shiffrin told Jayne, "Don't ever say you were dropped." Accordingly Jayne told the press, "My lawyer, Greg Bautzer, got offers for four pictures for me but I didn't want that. I asked Warner Brothers to release me because although everyone in Hollywood was saying, 'Jayne will be a

o o o o o o o o o o o o o o o o o o o o o o o o o o o o o o o o o o o o o o

big star someday, watch her go,' no one really did anything. So I came to New York and heard that Jules Styne
was looking for a Marilyn Monroe type for his show *Rock
Hunter*. I auditioned and got the part."

# *Success?*

JAYNE WENT to Philadelphia to shoot *The Burglar* after securing her part in *Will Success Spoil Rock Hunter? The Burglar* isn't much but it is one of the few movies in which
Jayne didn't play the usual. *"The Burglar* is very different
from anything I've ever done. It's a very serious role. No
make-up. No figure. They play down my bust. The
actress just has to come through. If they played up my
bust, it would detract from my acting. And I'm dramatic
rather than comic. I play the daughter of a thief who
shacks up with a good guy. It has a happy ending. I
marry the hero." Mansfield and Duryea didn't turn out to
have the electricity of Tracy and Hepburn, but there are
some nice shots of Atlantic City. Jayne's performance isn't
terrible. The role demanded that she display something
other than a pout and her breasts. Her obvious niceness
interferes with her portrayal of a tough girl. But the job
she did indicated that with some work and some direction
she might have become a passable actress.

Jayne made a quick trip to California before *Rock Hunter*
opened. She dropped in on Jerome Lipsky, a lawyer, who

o o o o o o o o o o o o o o o o o o o o o o o o o o o o o o o o o o o o o o

was then working with Greg Bautzer.  Lipsky, a tall, slender, understated man who handles numerous stars, now
works in an enormous leathered office in Beverly Hills.  He
has a dark, upholstered, circular waiting room that has the
feel of a costly padded cell.

Lipsky remembers Jayne coming to him on that visit and
saying, "Some lights fell on me while I was doing *The Burglar*.  Can I sue?"

"Were you hurt?" asked Lipsky.

"Yes.  It burned my right breast."

"Did it do any damage?"

"Yes, see?" whereupon Jayne pulled out her right breast
to demonstrate.

Lipsky said, "Excuse me for a minute."  As he explains,
"I had to get control of my giggles.  I said to a friend, 'I
may need some consultation on this one.'  I told the story
and immediately had five volunteers to come and look.  It
wasn't dirty.  You asked a question and she gave an answer.  She was a nice person, friendly and an exhibitionist."

Jayne had a lot of trouble keeping her clothes on, but
she, like Lipsky, thought it wasn't dirty.  Her attitude
about her nudity was quite matter of fact.  She knew men
would be shocked and momentarily undone.  That was the
effect she wanted.  She wasn't sultry or vampish.  That
level of sexuality required a sophistication she didn't in-
tend and one which conflicted with her image of the dumb
blonde.  She could take her clothes off, though, and men
would laugh and drool.  Lipsky giggled.  Jayne thought
that by making men laugh she was joining them in a joke
about sex.  She tried to keep her sexuality from threatening
by making it silly.  It was a way of being provocative and
simultaneously disowning the consequences.  If the audience was laughing it wasn't taking her seriously or blam-

ing her for being lewd. But the laughter was ribald and derisive and she, not sex, was the object.

The shooting schedule for *The Burglar* went overtime so the opening of *Rock Hunter* was held up. Sylvia Herscher, a shrewd and talented lady, was associate producer and manager of the show, a job she describes as, "doing it all and then cleaning it up." They were willing to wait for Jayne, she says, because "they had tried out lots of people and they couldn't find anyone with that particular quality." The play, which is a satire of the movie industry, stars a giggly, dizzy blonde, more or less based on the studio-stupid image of Marilyn Monroe. Jayne opened the show clad barely in a towel, lying on a massage table. Ms. Herscher was in Colorado during casting so when she returned Jayne was a fait accompli. "It was casting genius. I can't imagine anyone else doing the role. She didn't act the role, she *was* the role."

She first met Jayne while arranging some promotion deals with a furrier. Jayne was walking through the garment district with Ms. Herscher two steps behind. The garment workers were catcalling and whistling and Jayne was bowing and waving. "She loved it."

"I couldn't stand her," says Ms. Herscher candidly. I couldn't tolerate her behavior during rehearsals. She was always late and had no discipline." She admits that her feelings for Jayne were at least partly the result of management's attitude toward labor, but there was also a real personality rub between the two women. Ms. Herscher is a competent, hardworking woman who takes the theater and her work very seriously. Jayne, although she was also a hard worker, took neither the theater nor any one else's work seriously. She was in New York for fun, and she set out to have some.

"Actually," says Ms. Herscher, modifying her stand,

∘ ∘ ∘ ∘ ∘ ∘ ∘ ∘ ∘ ∘ ∘ ∘ ∘ ∘ ∘ ∘ ∘ ∘ ∘ ∘ ∘ ∘ ∘ ∘ ∘ ∘ ∘ ∘ ∘ ∘ ∘ ∘ ∘ ∘ ∘ ∘ ∘ ∘ ∘

"you couldn't dislike her.  She just always gave you a lot of trouble.  In the middle of rehearsals it got so bad that I finally called a meeting with Jayne and Marty Baum, Bill Schiffrin's New York representative, who was then acting as her agent.  I said unless she changed we were going to have to let her go.  I tried to put the fear of God into her.  I got up and said she could leave.  There was dead silence.  She turned green.  She shaped up for about three weeks."

To give Jayne credit, Ms. Herscher understands that "She'd never been to New York.  She'd never been on stage.  She had to exploit this time in New York.  She thought she was being sweet and adorable, but she wasn't.  She wasn't professional.  On the other hand, she had no stage fright, and she never lost her temper.  She'd say, 'I'll try, I'll be better.  I promise.'  She learned quickly enough and there weren't too many changes in the lines.  She was just a crazy lady."

The day she was to open, October 12, 1955, Jayne insisted on having a pedicure, manicure, facial and hairdo simultaneously.  She and Jim Byron necked in a cab all the way to the theater.  "We've got to neck," she said.  "It's the thing to do."

Management had an unusual opening night worry.  Sylvia Herscher had to plead with Marilyn Monroe not to come.  "There would be too much attention paid to her.  So she didn't come although she was very close to some of the members in the cast like Walter Matthau and Orson Bean."

Opening night was a glorious success.  Jayne wriggled around in her towel, and, although, as Shiffrin remarked, it was a lousy play, Jayne held it together.  Despite the resentment of Monroe's friends who, as Ms. Herscher recalls, weren't pleased that "that pipsqueak was keeping the play going," Jayne did just that.  To quote Shiffrin, "She killed them in New York."  The play ran for 452 perfor-

○ ○ ○ ○ ○ ○ ○ ○ ○ ○ ○ ○ ○ ○ ○ ○ ○ ○ ○ ○ ○ ○ ○ ○ ○ ○ ○ ○ ○ ○ ○ ○ ○ ○ ○ ○ ○ ○ ○ ○ ○

mances, closing only when Twentieth Century-Fox bought it to make the movie.

Ms. Herscher agreed with Shiffrin. "Jayne kept it alive by her own publicity. She did it herself. It didn't matter whether she had to stand on a mound of snow in ten below zero weather to sign autographs."

Troubles persisted between Jayne and management, but she was, after all, the star. Ms. Herscher remembers her getting to the theater at 8:25 for an 8:30 curtain. "She was supposed to wear a body stocking with the towel, but she didn't want to use the body stocking. She insisted on running around backstage nude. The stagehands were driving us crazy. Nobody could stand her. They'd be ready to kill when she came in late.

"In the opening scene, Jayne's feet were bare. When she would run on stage, the wardrobe mistress would have to run on stage, grab her and wash her feet. She had a dress that cost us a lot of money and she stuffed stockings into the bosom to make herself look bigger, distorting the dress.

"I once called a meeting, saying that there was a very serious problem, that backstage was a shambles. Since Jayne believed everything she read about herself in the papers, I said I was going to place an item in the papers saying that Jayne is never late, has impeccable deportment backstage. She was a doll for three months."

After that Ms. Herscher had regular sessions with Jayne, who would straighten out for some weeks. But she was too full of herself to behave for long.

Except for the talking-tos, Jayne was having a wonderful time. She was the star she was playing. She had fans. People all over New York recognized her. She appeared in the columns almost every day. The press loved her. She was a sensation.

Ken Baxter, a Hollywood press agent, used to skip school

when he was fifteen and hang around the stage door at *Rock Hunter*. He met Jayne, got her autograph and kept going back. They eventually became good friends. After one performance he went backstage and Jayne said she wanted to go out and buy records. She was wearing bright red toreador pants, a very low-cut leopard-skin blouse, a mink coat slung over her shoulders and backless Springolator heels. "As we went down Broadway, every single head turned. I was very proud. Jayne," he said with affection, "looked terrible. Her hair was a brassy blond, she wore black eyebrow pencil with the top line and bottom line all joined together and bright red lipstick."

Baxter says Jayne was "marvelous. She was awfully kind to her fans. She began to know everyone by name and took an interest in them. She never brushed anyone off but waited patiently till the last one had his autograph."

Jayne said, "I run on a publicity schedule like a train. The boys line up something, tell me where to go and what to wear and I go. Then I go someplace else and pose again. I make speeches, commentate fashion shows, anything."

The publicist for *Rock Hunter* was John B. Toohey. His schedule for Jayne covering four days in June of 1956 reads like this.

Tuesday, June 12
12:30 P.M. be at Belasco ready to leave for Monmouth racetrack. Norm Rettig is out of town, and will be until late tomorrow afternoon, so I won't be able to get him to send a special car.
If you're back from the racetrack in time, Bronzini is having a party from 5:30 to 7:30 at 5 East 52nd Street. They've picked the "50 best-dressed men in New York," and if you care to show up for pictures, they'll be glad to take some. After the show Harry Dorman is having a housewarming at 80 Park Avenue and you are cordially invited.

Wednesday, June 13
After the show, Norm Rettig (who'll be back in town by then)

will send a limousine to the theatre to take you over to Madison Square Garden, for a bow at the Cavalcade of the Stars.

Thursday, June 14
At noon you will be picked up at the Gorham and taken (by Joan Crosby) to Sherry's Restaurant, 270 Park Avenue, for lunch. Sherry's ran some sort of contest about getting men to name the person they'd most like to have lunch with. The man who won the contest picked you. He has something like six sons, all of whom will be with him, and you should have a lot of fun.
After the show you will be picked up by Captain Sid Burns of the Civil Air Patrol and driven out to Brooklyn for a couple of pictures with some beauty contest winners, and then driven right back to the city. You should be back in Manhattan by 12:15 or 12:30.

Friday, June 15
IMPORTANT: Friday is left entirely open to *Life*.

Jayne and *Life* worked together on a number of spreads, but the happiest collaboration resulted in an article published in April 1956 by Ernest Havemann. He had sympathy, humor and understanding for Jayne and what she was trying to do. He captured her deliberately witless charm and was generous in setting her up with straight lines.

Havemann: "Do you like to cook?"
Jayne: "Every once in a while I like to put on dungarees and a plaid shirt and cook up some bacon and eggs. I can also cook turkeys. They're so good when they're cooked, you know."

Jayne went on to describe her friend and astrologer David Sturgis. Sturgis was a Leo and insisted that Jayne's career be guided by Leos. Besides his astrological talents, Sturgis was a playwright. He had written a play called *The Loon*. Jayne summarized, "There's a bird upstairs and a couple of halfwits running around and a man with dirt under his fingernails.  It's very mysterious; I loved what I read of it."

Bill Shiffrin, whom Havemann also interviewed, was not so enchanted with Sturgis.  Jayne said, "I keep telling Bill that Mr. Sturgis used to advise Duse and Nijinsky and all kinds of people like that but Bill just says, 'All dead people.'  Well, I admit Nijinsky came to a bad end, but he was very big while he had it."

When Jayne told Havemann about *The Loon*, she neglected to tell him the circumstances under which she had come not to finish it.  Sturgis (who later became a guru to the first wave of flower children in the Haight) and Jayne met in Los Angeles.  He told her about the play just before she went to New York.  She asked Shiffrin to read it and assured him, sight unseen, that it was marvelous.  Bill found the play so execrable that he thought, "Maybe Jayne's putting me on."  He called Jayne the next time she was in California, said he read the play and that it was "brilliant, absolutely brilliant.  You've got to come over and we'll read it."  He then read it aloud to her slowly until she was helpless with laughter.  Shiffrin says, "I was trying to straighten her out.  I'd buy Sturgis dinner, but I told him to get out of her life.  I didn't want him to exploit or destroy her."

Sturgis helped provide Jayne with some of the best copy she was ever to get.  The *Life* article was close to the high point of her publicity career, only she didn't understand it.  She knew the publicity was good because it was *Life*, but she didn't capitalize on the zany character she was creating for herself.  She was genuinely funny, but she was never allowed to become a real comedienne.  Laughter dampens sexual interest and Jayne's advisers were afraid that if she got too funny, she'd stop being sexy.  Her humor had to refer to her body or her stupidity or she confused her audience, which expected only one kind of laugh out of her.

o o o o o o o o o o o o o o o o o o o o o o o o o o o o o o o o o o o o

Jayne took her publicity where she could find it. As Ms. Herscher put it, "She'd get up early in the morning and drag herself out to the Bayside supermarket opening. She was the queen of the supermarkets. There wasn't a supermarket in New York she didn't open that year."

One of Jayne's more extended publicity stunts at the time involved Count Stefano V. Tirone, whom she met at several Broadway parties. Jayne sketched one of their encounters. "He met me backstage and brushed my ear with his lips and kissed my hands and said, 'You are so beautiful, so lovely, so gorgeous. I love you so much. Why don't we get married? Why don't you be my wife? Why are you so cold to me?' I told him, 'Oh, Stephie, don't be such a roué.' "

A few weeks later the unlucky count crashed his car against a stone wall and died. It was revealed that he was not a count at all, but Stephen Vlabovith, an impoverished Yugoslavian, sexton of the Church of St. Mary's of the Isle in Long Beach, New York. He left a wife and two children. Jayne wanted to have her picture taken kissing the brow of the dead man. She had a falling out with her friend Broadway press agent George Bennett, who said the idea was ghoulish. Jayne prevailed.

Charlsa remembers her first encounter with Jayne in New York. "Four years had gone by and Jayne was a big star. I thought some day I'll get in touch with her, but I'm not going to barge in on her success. But I was walking down the street one night and there she was. I couldn't get over all this white strawlike hair. I screamed, 'Jaynie' and she turned around. She said, 'Charlsa' and we ran and threw our arms around each other. Meanwhile all of a sudden out of nowhere there were photographers taking our picture. That's what she had hanging around her all the time.

"She worked herself into just a tizzy. She was doing

o o o o o o o o o o o o o o o o o o o o o o o o o o o o o o o o o o o o

two shows a day. She'd be up all night, she'd give interviews and they'd want her to come to a dinner. She was on the run all the time. I remember saying, 'Jaynie, you've got to get some rest.' She said to me, 'Charlsa, these are not my resting years.' It was almost like she was forecasting something."

Since Charlsa had met her last, Jayne's ambition had found its expression. She told Sylvia Herscher that she wanted to have a house in Beverly Hills, have a million dollars and be a star. "She was very frank about what she wanted."

Ann Wedgeworth, who encountered her in New York, was dumfounded at Jayne's matter-of-fact confidence. Jayne was doing the play, she told Ann, "because it will help me in my climb to the top."

Jayne was beginning to collect star-accouterments, tangible proof to document her success. The first thing she wanted was a Jaguar. She consulted Byron and he advised her to wait on such a big expense. But Jayne stamped her foot and said, "I want that car and I'm going to have that goddamned car." Byron called Bautzer who said, characteristically, "Beautiful girls should have beautiful things." Jayne got the car and had it painted pink. As Byron says, "She drove the ass off that car." It always figured among her favorite things. "I love candlelight, music, artistic things, squirrels, and rabbits, my Great Dane and my pink Jaguar."

During her Broadway stint Jayne promoted furs, dresses, jewels and the like. She had a powerful aversion to spending money. As Sylvia Herscher says, "She promoted everything but rent. She promoted having her hair done at Larry Matthews' studio. She never once tipped an operator. She was not generous, which is so unusual in the theater where everyone is so generous. She had her wardrobe mistress working her back off for her. She did all the work, baby-sat for Jayne Marie, took all her dumb phone calls and after a year's run, Jayne gave her a dollar. I thought she would have a fit."

Jayne didn't like to spend, but she did like to have. It wasn't greed so much as a childlike insecurity. The trappings of being a star were a kind of positive identification of who she was. She wrote Byron pleading letters saying, Make me a star, make me a star. In the same vein she said, "My hair is naturally brown, but I look more like what people think a movie star should look like when it's this moonlight color." She went around in ninety-degree heat dragging a mink behind her. Her explanation to movie director Frank Tashlin was, "I'm trying to appear casual. I want people to think I'm used to mink."

Jayne's first real success brought on a wave of anxiety to succeed bigger. As Byron says, "She wanted success but never felt she had it. It drove her to keep moving all the time." She was hyperactive, promoting herself day and night. But every morning she'd wake up and feel that she still hadn't made it, that she still had to become a star. That self-doubt was built in from the start, built into the role she had planned for herself. There was no way for Jayne to relax when her career rested on her personality. Her job and her personality coincided perfectly in *Rock Hunter* and in a couple of movies she made afterward. But because she and the industry couldn't think beyond dumb blonde, she could only become more and more exaggerated.

During this frenzied year she didn't have a lot of time for Jayne Marie. She and her daughter lived in a small apartment in the Gorham on West 55th Street. It was a one-bedroom suite with no doors. Ms. Herscher said Jayne used to send the girl "to play in the subway at Fifty-fifth

Street. She'd skip up and down the steps. She never gave the kid any attention." Jayne often used Ken Baxter to baby-sit as well as her wardrobe mistress.

In spite of her overwhelming schedule, Jayne did try and see as much of her little girl as possible. She even took her along on dates. Jayne Marie would sit in the ladies' room while her mother had a drink with an admirer. As she put it, "My mother takes me lots of places with her."

It was a confusing life for the child, but she was sweet and docile and terribly proud of her mother. Ken Baxter took her to a matinee of *That Certain Feeling*. Later they went to the automat. A woman sat down next to them, turned to Jayne Marie and said, "Oh, aren't you cute." Jayne Marie replied that yes, she was and that, "My mommy's a star on Broadway." Jayne loved her daughter's devotion. It was as if her child gave her the kind of uncritical approval she never got from Vera. As the child grew older, their roles reversed in a number of ways.

Jayne, like Vera, was a demanding mother, but only when she thought about it. Unlike Vera, her demands had more to do with how Jayne Marie responded to her than with external behavior or achievements. The little girl fell asleep during one of the countless performances of *Rock Hunter* which she attended. Jayne cautioned her afterward. "How do you expect to grow up and become a great actress if you don't watch your mother?" Jayne was less interested in her daughter's stage career than she was in her complete involvement and adulation.

It was a peculiar atmosphere for a small child. William Mishkin, then a reporter for *Look*, found the girl disturbingly precocious, mimicking her mother's sexy mannerisms. Jayne warmed to the flattery implied by the imitation. Jayne Marie instinctively knew what was expected of her. As she grew older she became Jayne's assistant hairdresser, wardrobe mistress and bartender. In some fundamental ways she came to mother Jayne, and Jayne depended on her to do so.

Another important element in their relationship was the fact that it was 1955 and Jayne was a working mother. Working mothers were, by definition, bad mothers. They were selfish and irresponsible. They weren't home after school to nag their children about practicing the piano. Their children were without guidance and they were responsible for that new postwar disease, juvenile delinquency. So, whether it seemed appropriate or advisable, Jayne always wanted her children with her. She couldn't give them attention but she could give them proximity. Jayne had to prove to herself and Vera that she could work and be a good mother at the same time, even when it involved taking her daughter out on her dates and out of school to travel all over the world with her.

Meanwhile, Jayne was conducting as active a social life as her schedule and energies would allow. She was pleased to give reporters insights about the kind of man she would marry. "He must be artistic, must have succeeded in his field, must be an exciting strong personality. It would help if he had charcoal gray hair and blue eyes, but brown eyes would be all right. I prefer men between the ages of forty-eight and fifty."

Jayne had a number of flings left over from California. Steve Cochran, a neighboring performer on Wanda Park Drive, was "particularly attractive because of his ruggedness. Steve is casual at all times. If a girl proposed to him he could say 'no' so easily that no one could be embarrassed or frustrated. He has the he-man charm that women fall for. He doesn't rely on techniques." Jayne was also seeing director Nicholas Ray, whose films include *Rebel Without a Cause.* And Jayne remained intimate with

o o o o o o o o o o o o o o o o o o o o o o o o o o o o o o o o o o o o

Jim Byron on the long-distance phone late at night. She would regale him with stories about losing her diaphragm at inopportune moments.

Then there was Robby Robertson, in whom Jayne found the requisite charcoal gray, but not in his eyes. Robertson was an airline pilot. "He's six feet tall with dark brown eyes and charcoal gray hair. I feel so companionable and safe with him. He's sympathetic and understanding."

She met Robertson on a plane in April 1955. "All the other men including some pilots were making these huge pitches, but when he walked through the plane — he was flying it — I thought, 'I've got to have this.' He's the only person in my whole life I ever gave my phone number to the first time he asked for it."

After that unprecedented libertinism she admitted, "I've been infatuated with quite a few but there aren't any others who are so perfectly made for me and who I'm so perfectly made for. He's so very handsome and he's got that wonderful hair, and he's willing to go along with my career. He wants me to be the biggest thing since Jean Harlow. This is just a beautiful thing and when I go out with anybody else I say, 'Why am I doing this?' "

By all accounts Robby was a very nice man, a little dull, handsome in a canine sort of way and very straight. Charlsa met him at Jayne's several times. "I liked Robby. A very nice guy. He was smart and had Jaynie's best interest at heart. I remember he was looking at some pictures Jaynie had taken for a layout. They were pinup pictures. And some of them were not in the best of taste. There were a lot of them and she had the first say-so. She could scratch out the ones that were not . . . And he really was strict, 'No, you can't have that one,' and she really got kind of angry with him.

"I said are you going to marry him, and she never was very committal about him. So, I don't think her heart was really in the relationship at all. I think he loved her and wanted the best for her, but I don't think that was Jaynie's kind of guy."

One of Robby's drawbacks was his very high speaking voice. Jayne couldn't use an escort whose parts weren't perfect and a big strong man with a high little voice just didn't work. But, more important, Robby wanted to control what she did and she was having none of it. Paul had wanted her to come back home to Texas and now Robby wanted her to cut the cheesecake. In both cases Jayne dropped the men along with their suggestions. Robby later married and widowed Linda Darnell.

Paul Mansfield, who was at this time working in public relations for the Union Pacific Railroad, had begun proceedings to get custody of Jayne Marie on the grounds that Jayne was an unfit mother. The basis of the suit was that Jayne had posed almost nude for the February issue of *Playboy,* 1956. She also posed for the February 1955 issue of *Playboy,* but Paul seemed not to have noticed.

Jayne said, "I'm a very stainless character, my petticoats are clean. I read little Bible stories to Jayne Marie every night and she is a well-balanced and intelligent child. Those pictures in *Playboy* magazine I posed for to get milk and bread for the baby." It appears unlikely that this was the case since Jayne was making about $1250 a week from *Rock Hunter* and her personal appearances.

Paul said, "I don't want a million men looking at my wife."

Jayne said, "That's part of being a star."

Jayne had filed for separate maintenance in 1955 and amended it to divorce the following year. Jerome Lipsky handled the proceedings and says they were "routine." The custody suit, however, stung Jayne, since it threatened her with bad press. She attacked. "Paul refused to support me in a style compatible with nonstarvation. Because my husband did not make enough to pay household bills, I had to work for bread and butter money." He objected to her working. "He wanted to keep me in the kitchen" (presumably to cook that turkey) "from five A.M. to five P.M. Paul had such jobs as sweeping out the grocery, to selling cement, to selling radio time, to selling vibrators." She unloaded another heartfelt grievance: "Paul thought my Chihuahua was taking my attachment away from him and he wanted me to get rid of it."

Jayne's interpretation of the whole thing was that Paul still wanted her back and making trouble was the best way of doing it. She said in March 1956, "He was so jealous of my career. He calls up every so often and cries for me to go back to him. This is his last contact with me and I guess he's going the whole hog." She said later, just before the divorce was complete, "I won't have any trouble. My husband is very much in love with me, and he'll give me my divorce. What he really wants is for me to come back to him."

Vera still hears from Paul every now and then and feels he has always been in love with Jayne. Despite this handicap he has managed to remarry, father four children and settle down as a public relations man and devout Baptist. People close to him say those years with Jayne were "the worst in his life and he wants to forget them entirely."

Jayne, he said, caused him "pain, anguish and distress."

She said, "I have no idea why he would say such a thing. All I can say is, I hope he has fun." Judge Samuel R. Blake granted the Mansfields a divorce on October 24, 1956, on the grounds of Paul's extreme mental cruelty. Jayne retained custody of her daughter. Paul was charged with twenty dollars a month child support and one dollar a month token alimony.

Jayne had expanded her ambitions. She no longer found it glamorous to be married to an older man, a college man.

o o o o o o o o o o o o o o o o o o o o o o o o o o o o o o o o o o o o o o o

She had created her own life and Paul gave her cabin fever. He could never supply the things she could now offer herself. Her problem with Paul echoed in other relationships. She never found a man who could do more for her than she and her imagination could do for herself. She metabolized excitement very fast and constantly demanded new injections.

Charlsa thinks, "If she'd met a Mike Todd type when she was young and she'd married him, I think that probably she would have given up her career without any question. After a few years of that glamor I think she probably would not have been willing to give it up for something else. Jaynie had to have somebody she was in love with. I mean that was one thing she couldn't compromise."

Being in love was the single most sustaining force in Jayne's life. It meant something heady, full of props and extras, a blend of emotions, libido, fantasy and trappings. She wanted to be in love, not in any down-home garden variety way, but complete with moon, candles, violins, minks, champagne and Jaguars. It wasn't an original vision, but the relentlessness with which she pursued it was. Bryon recalls how she always felt she might be missing something. "She never felt she had enough time to do everything. It expressed itself in eating. She would devour her own food, Jaynie Marie's and mine. She did everything that way. She even made love that way."

Author Jim Bishop wrote after her death, "To her sex and the human male formed a stairway. All she had to do was climb it." But the point about Jayne was not that she was ambitious as men commonly define it. Her strongest desires had to do with what are most often the side effects of ambition for men. She wanted rapturous love, not a sex object, but a romance-object, a man who would outdistance her and be more to her than she was to herself. Her career, as she saw it, was simply a backdrop for a love affair. She never expected that her career would become her most stable love affair.

Jayne had that year the thrilling example of Grace Kelly's wedding to Prince Rainier to rev up her imagination, but Jayne didn't need encouragement in the fantasy department. Her high school training helped her inflate infatuations into love, tricking herself into momentary optimism. Sometimes she fantacized about famous men. Even Adlai Stevenson wasn't exempt. "He is a strong powerful man and so sure of himself. I admire his strength of character. I'd like to know him." She had to be in love to function on that frenetic level which characterized her. She was always ready. She fooled herself most of the time, but she came closest to what she wanted when she met Mickey Hargitay.

# *Mickey*

♥ ♥ ♥

ON MAY 26, 1956, Jayne and Jules Styne, composer and producer of *Rock Hunter*, went to the Latin Quarter after Jayne's performance. They watched Mae West and her seven enormous men. Jayne was particularly taken with one of the chorus boys and asked Styne to introduce him. Styne obliged and soon Jayne was sitting with ex–Mr. Universe Mickey Hargitay. In those days Mickey was abundantly muscled, weighed two hundred and thirty pounds and stood six-two. He had brown curly hair which he wore longish in the front and greased in the back. He had pointy white teeth, a pointed nose, thin lips and a Victor Mature smile. His Hungarian accent was much richer then than it is now, causing him to substitute v's for w's and wice wersa. Jayne and Mickey didn't have too long to talk between sets that night, but it was long enough to exchange phone numbers and size each other up. "Mickey has a fifty-two-inch chest expansion and I measure over forty inches and we both have short arms. All this makes dancing difficult."

Jayne told Mickey that she lived in the Gorham and

worried all the way home that he misunderstood and thought she said the Gotham. He was on the phone when she got home, however, and they made a date for the next morning. That night Mae got angry at Mickey for being on the floor between performances with Jayne. It deflected attention from Mae, who wanted Hargitay for herself. She ceased introducing him as the "most perfectly built man in the world."

The following morning, Jayne and Mickey showed up in Brooklyn where Jayne was crowned Blossom Queen. Mickey and she cooed and nuzzled for the delighted photographers. The next day they were all over the front page of the *Daily News*. They had fallen in love. Mae was not amused. She threatened to fire Mickey if he didn't renounce Jayne. Mae's entourage trooped up to Syracuse. Mickey spent his last night with Jayne, called her for hours on end from Syracuse and spent a couple of days with her in the Catskills before Mae's act opened in Washington.

Mickey was turning out to be great publicity. He rejoined Mae West in Washington. She was enraged with him for his romance and the coverage he and Jayne were getting. She told him that she'd called a press conference after the show in which he was to say that everything between him and Jayne was pure publicity and he wasn't going to see her anymore.

Mickey showed up at the press conference and declared that he was very much in love with Jayne and that they had serious plans. Ross Christena, Mickey's friend and manager from Indianapolis, gives a blow-by-blow description of the ensuing spectacle. "Chuck Krauser, Mae's bodyguard, set upon Mickey from behind. It was a sneak attack. Krauser jumped Mickey, knocked me down and tore off my shirt. Then Mr. America sat on Krauser and Mae got knocked down. She sat on the floor and said,

o o o o o o o o o o o o o o o o o o o o o o o o o o o o o o o o o o o o

'You can't do this to me. I'm an institution.' We took Krauser to court and he was fined for assault."

Mickey explained the sabotage. "I was attacked without knowing it. I looked away. It was the first time in my life I ever got hit.

"Ever since I been in the Mae West show she has exhibited great affection for me. She wanted to replace this other guy who had been her boyfriend for a year with me. But I fell for Jayne when I met her in New York recently. Mae was jealous.

"It was a very sneaky way to attack somebody. I don't think it makes me any smaller. I'm even feel bigger now."

Jayne was "thrilled about the way Mickey handled Krauser. Mickey has intelligence and breeding and he controls his animalistic tendencies."

Mae called Mickey "the old Mr. Universe, last year's model."

Mickey replied ungallantly, "I think that's funny. If I'm the old model, then who is she?"

Jayne, ever trying to be fair, observed, "I've always been told to respect my elders. She's sixty-four, and if I look that good at sixty-four, I'll have no problems whatever. I look upon her as a fabulous entertainer."

The incident gave Jayne and Mickey a chance to be together permanently, since Mae fired Mickey, who flew to New York where photographers shot him with a bandage over his left eye, holding Jayne in a halter-necked red dress, tight as a tourniquet. The couple commented on their relationship.

"We feel very strong for each other," said Mickey.

"Ever since I met him two weeks ago I just knew he was the greatest," said Jayne.

Mickey came to this country in 1947 when he was seventeen. He left Budapest to escape the Russian draft and landed in Brooklyn with ten dollars and "a happy smile on my face." His first job was in a fruit market in Brooklyn working for two dollars a day. He moved to Indianapolis where he met and married Mary Birge. When he wasn't being a carpenter, Mickey put together an adagio dance act with Mary. Adagio dancing is slow and athletic, involving much heaving and flinging about. It resembles Apache dancing. Mickey had had some experience on the stage in Budapest with Yolanda Birge, his cousin, who was married to Donald Birge, Mary's brother, a GI stationed in Budapest. Yolanda came to this country with her husband and replaced Mary in the dance act when Mary gave birth to Tina Hargitay in 1949. Mickey and Yolanda never made much of a success out of adagio dancing, but Mickey met the man who helped him get to Mae West. Ross Christena, a medium-sized man with a Roman haircut, now balding, met Mickey in Indianapolis. He calls himself an artist's manager and was responsible for booking dates for both Jayne and Mickey.

In 1955 Mickey, who had developed a serious interest in body building, entered and won the Mr. Universe contest at the Palladium theater in London. It was this achievement which brought him to Mae West's attention and put him in her chorus line.

Body building in the fifties wasn't as exotic as it is now. In those days Mickey was what high school girls used to call a real hunk, referring to his stature, not his origins. It was a period when people didn't have bodies: men had physiques and girls had figures. The style for men was definitely brutish.

Jayne was crazy about Mickey. She saw them as the perfect couple, a matched set of astounding bodies. An heroic couplet. His body was terribly important to her, sexually and symbolically. He wasn't all that forceful or distinguished, but his bulk made him someone to reckon with.

o o o o o o o o o o o o o o o o o o o o o o o o o o o o o o o o o o o o o

Jayne could wrap him around her pinkie, but he could pick
her up with his. And she loved how she saw them, how
she thought other people saw them. She made sure that
they were seen. They even took to making love at parties.

Charlsa remembers, "She would just stand there and she
would always be kissing him and he would always be kissing her. You know they just loved each other." Mickey
was like a toy for Jayne. She loved to get him to flex and
perform. He obediently went through his paces, picking
her up, pressing her, pleased that she was pleased.

Mickey could hardly believe his good fortune when
Jayne fell in love with him. He thought she was the most
beautiful, exciting, sexy woman in the world. He wasn't
trying to use her for anything, change her or exploit her in
any way. Charlsa says, ". . . he thought anything she did
was just great. Mickey let her do anything she wanted to.
And he was so sweet." Sylvia Herscher agrees. "He
wasn't using her or taking her. He just had a genuine ap-
preciation of her."

Mickey's critics like to point out his failures. He succeeded, however, at making Jayne happy for a while. His
secret was extreme passivity under the guise of total in-
dulgence. Ken Baxter remembers him "following her
around like an overprotective teddy bear. He tolerated everything, stood back and smiled at all her friends and her
life-style. It was an 'Oh, have your fun' attitude." Mickey
provided the quiet, supermasculine presence, and Jayne
provided the excitement. The umbrella of Jayne's fantasy
life was plenty big enough for two, and she held it over
Mickey for a long time. He was docile and unprotesting
and became, therefore, many of the things she dreamed up
for him. The ideal romance object.

Like everything else Jayne loved, Mickey was an exag-
geration. He was larger than life with his rippling dorsals
and pectorals. She loved outlandish clothes, outrageous

○ ○ ○ ○ ○ ○ ○ ○ ○ ○ ○ ○ ○ ○ ○ ○ ○ ○ ○ ○ ○ ○ ○ ○ ○ ○ ○ ○ ○ ○ ○ ○ ○ ○ ○ ○ ○ ○ ○

exploits and all things camp. And Mickey was nothing, if not camp.

As time went on Jayne and Mickey reversed most traditional male-female roles. Jayne's career came first, Jayne's demands came first. She thoroughly controlled him. He was doglike in his devotion to her. He came backstage with flowers, carried her coat, took care of Jayne Marie and waited around when she was busy elsewhere. He was living with her from the time he lost his job with Mae West and busied himself with her affairs.

He did have ambitions of a sort. Jayne explained, "Mickey wants to do more with his life than just show his body. Anybody can do that." Mickey wanted to be an actor, although, as it turned out, his real talents lay in construction work.

Jayne was a willful woman who got her way. Mickey was so enchanted with her in the beginning that their wishes always coincided. If they didn't, Mickey backed down, because he was afraid of damaging their relationship and angering Jayne.

Jayne said, "I'm that way about Mickey because he's a sincere, sweet, lovable guy and not because he has such an outstanding physique." On the contrary, Jayne loved that outstanding physique to distraction. But she also loved her idea of Mickey, and it was into his void that she poured all of her imaginative and creative energies, making theirs a wide-screen, Technicolor romance. Mickey is a conservative, stubborn man, suspicious by nature. He is not flighty, but found himself fascinated by her snake-charming ways and her daring. She supplied him with intravenous energy and provoked him out of his sluggishness. She kissed the lumbering Hungarian and he woke up an American prince, 1956 model. Jayne had no cynicism about the affair. She had found true love and it was going to make her happy. The force of her commitment

o o o o o o o o o o o o o o o o o o o o o o o o o o o o o o o o o o o o o o o o o

moved Mickey, propelled him to romantic heights he'd
never imagined.

All this happened very fast. Jayne and Mickey were in
love three days after they met. Vera was interviewed in
Dallas in July when Jayne and Mickey had been smooching
for the press for six weeks. "Now all those stories about
Jaynie and that fellow in Mae West's act. He was just
using Jaynie to get himself some publicity. She picked
him out of a chorus line." Vera and Harry were not prepared to like Mickey. They got their chance in August
when they came to New York. To their surprise they
found him "charming," although the trip wasn't. At a
party they met a fast-talking promoter, who swindled them
out of $10,000, claiming he was going to invest it in quick-
profit hospital beds. The Peerses went back to Dallas
poorer and more worldly. As for Mickey, it took some
years for relations between him and Vera to disintegrate to
the point when she dumped a restaurant table in his lap
for "deviling Jaynie." They now find Mickey "full of guff."

In the spring of 1956 Jayne's agent, Bill Shiffrin, read the
script for *The Girl Can't Help It*. Frank Tashlin, who
directed the movie, wanted Jayne to play the lead. Shiffrin's first idea was to get Tashlin to postpone the movie
until *Rock Hunter* completed its run. But Tashlin was im-
patient, so he suggested that Tashlin do *Rock Hunter* as a
film, changing the story so it didn't reflect badly on the
movie industry. Then Fox could buy and close the play
and make both movies. Fox bought the play for $125,000
and Jayne came home.

George Axelrod, author and producer of *Rock Hunter*,
gave a final party for the cast, distributing, in innocence of
the consequences, heart-shaped silver key rings to all
members of the production. Since Jayne accurately
regarded Axelrod as an intellectual she adopted his heart-
shaped motif as her very own. Her bathtub, swimming

pool, bed and decorations all subsequently became heart-shaped, as did the dots over her i's.

Throughout her run on Broadway, Jayne had been urged by Shiffrin not to sign a contract with one of the studios. Fox offered her a salary of $1000 a week, and Shiffrin said, "Don't be stupid. They're all creeps. Don't worry about a contract. You can emerge from this play at one hundred thousand dollars a picture." Fox continued to try to tempt Jayne. Shiffrin repeated his pitch for independence. "Look, it would be dumb to sign the Fox contract. They'll ruin you. They never follow through. They can't. The corporation is too big. It's a tough place to deal with. You're a star. You don't need a contract."

Jayne didn't believe Shiffrin, although she postponed signing with any studio for a few months. She couldn't bear the insecurity of not having a salary or the possibility of idleness. An agent is inevitably more patient, fore-sighted and daring than a client can afford to be and Jayne wanted immediate results. So Fox bought her for $1250 a week.

Jayne and Mickey flew back to California at the end of August. Jayne described her reentry to Hedda Hopper. "Mickey just happened to be on the plane with me. That part of my arrival was accidental; but having all my pets on hand to greet me was prearranged. I believe in flashy entrances. I've been going with Mickey in New York and he had movie offers and came out to take advantage of them. He's sweet and intelligent and probably the most unusual person I know." Mickey's movie offers at that point consisted in a part which had been written in for him in the film version of *Rock Hunter*.

Mickey wasn't the only surprise on Jayne's flight. Buddy Adler, executive producer of Twentieth Century-Fox, was there too. Jayne said, "I was traveling incognito.

I did my hair up, tied my head in a black scarf, put on some huge dark glasses and wrapped myself in a mink so nobody would know I was a movie star. Now I hear Mr. Adler was there and had told the studio not to meet him. He didn't want to interfere with my camera entrance. I think that was just too sweet."

It was good business, too. Fox encouraged Jayne to dream up her own entrances, stunts and publicity campaigns. The studio, by and large, was an interested observer rather than a participant in Jayne's publicity. The age had passed, and, as Shiffrin said, the studio was just too big to do much for its employees. Fox did have one dubious idea for Jayne. They suggested Jayne and Mickey stage a fight, after which Jayne would fall in love with "a Charles Van Doren type intellectual." Jayne was haughty about the proposal and refused on the grounds that Mickey, shy and introverted as he was, "wouldn't approve of the public display."

# The Girl Can't Help It

♥ ♥ ♥

JAYNE AND MICKEY settled down in the Wanda Park Drive house, which became known as Jayne's honeymoon cottage. While Jayne started getting Jayne Marie ready for school and enrolling her in the Beverly Hills All Saints Episcopal Sunday school, Mickey started building Jayne's swimming pool.

Bill Shiffrin drove Jayne to the Fox studios for her first day of work. It was Jaynie Marie's first day of school and Jayne asked Bill to pick them both up and drop the little girl off at school. After Jayne Marie left the car, Jayne started to cry.

"What's the matter?" asked Bill.

"God, I feel like such a mother," said Jayne as if it had never occurred to her before.

The next moment she wanted to get some breakfast. Before they sat down to eat Jayne said, "I've got to get some papers."

"Why?"

"To see if there are notices of my arrival." Fortunately

○ ○ ○ ○ ○ ○ ○ ○ ○ ○ ○ ○ ○ ○ ○ ○ ○ ○ ○ ○ ○ ○ ○ ○ ○ ○ ○ ○ ○ ○ ○ ○ ○ ○ ○ ○ ○ ○

the coverage was good, so she and Bill went off happily to buy Jayne a comb and go to the studio. She was starring in *The Girl Can't Help It* with Tom Ewell. The script was remotely based on a story by Garson Kanin called *Do-Re-Mi*. When director Frank Tashlin was finished there was nothing left of Kanin's story. Kanin refused to take a screen credit for the film. Buddy Adler, amazed at Kanin's refusal, offered his own wisdom. "Listen," he told Kanin, "we bought your story and we made a picture out of it, and we can still make a picture out of it."

*The Girl Can't Help It* is a witless comedy about an impossibly constructed woman who is being forced, against her wishes, into show business by her protector, an aging gangster. Aging gangster hires a once famous, now down and out agent to make Jayne a success. The agent, Tom Ewell, is haunted by sexy memories of Julie London who keeps appearing to him in visions, huskily singing in his dreams.

It is the juxtaposition of the sultry vamp and the innocent sex kitten. Julie London's powerful and mature sexuality can't compete with the springlike appeal of the girl-woman Jayne. Ewell starts out more innocent than Julie and less innocent than Jayne. He is reclaimed from his lingering despair and cynicism by Jayne's virginal nature, confiding ways and lisping voice. Julie acknowledges and uses sex, while Jayne pretends it isn't there. Jayne's charms recall Ewell from the brink of alcoholism.

Jayne weaves down the street and milk bottles explode. She walks through a restaurant and waiters drop their trays. Even the little paperboy is panting after her. The combination of her gigantic breasts and her sweet untouched personality makes her lethal. Basically she wants to sit home and make omelets for Tom Ewell but her sexuality keeps interfering. It is *The Captain's Paradise* paradox, in which Alec Guinness plays a bigamist who undoes himself by keeping his tango-inclined wife in the kitchen and his domestic wife out on the town.

The sexual innuendoes in *The Girl Can't Help It* are gross and childish. Men's eyes pop out and sweat pours down their foreheads. They elbow each other in the ribs, exchange winks, make lewd remarks and then talk to Jayne as if she were a member of the Salvation Army. The assumption is, of course, that women, poor dears, don't know how dangerous they are, how dangerous sex is. Women must be protected from their sexuality. Jayne played the Typhoid Mary of sex, a carrier, but never infected with desire.

Fats Domino, Little Richard and Gene Vincent are responsible for the best scenes in the movie. It's curious to see how uncomfortable Jayne was with rock 'n' roll. She was much more at home with tinkly cocktail music than with the hard rhythmic, overtly sexual sounds of early rock 'n' roll.

After completing *The Girl Can't Help It,* Jayne went on to shoot perhaps her most creditable performance in *The Wayward Bus.* The screenplay was by John Steinbeck and the action takes place on a bus which breaks down. Jayne does fairly well as one of the passengers. Shiffrin was pleased that Jayne took the part. He kept trying to steer her away from being cast as "another giggly blonde." He had some unrealized ideas for Jayne, including the lead in Dorothy Parker's "Big Blonde." He almost got Jayne what would become Lee Remick's role in *Anatomy of a Murder.* As Shiffrin puts it, "Remick was too patrician. Jayne would have been wonderful. She was blowsy, a real *broad.*" Shiffrin would have typecast Jayne in another stereotype, equally demeaning. But, at the time, anything, he felt, was better than another giggly blonde.

At the very beginning of 1957, Jayne's grandfather, Elmer Palmer, died in Pen Argyl. His house was held in trust for Jayne and the rest of the inheritance came to about $90,000, including $30,000 in real estate, $25,000 in personal property and the remainder of Mrs. Palmer's estate.

Fox began shooting *Rock Hunter* that winter. Tashlin adapted the script so that it would satirize television rather than the frightened movie industry. As in a number of films from that period, there is a short intermission in the story, bringing audiences a little message ridiculing television and urging people to support motion pictures. The other change Tashlin made was in writing in a small part for Mickey. He was cast as Jayne's lover, the star of a TV jungle series. He gets to beat up on Tony Randall, Jayne's pretend lover. Mickey's performance was vigorous.

When she finished the movie Jayne went on the Ed Sullivan show. She played the violin with six male violinists backing her. As one of them put it, "This is amazing. The violin is very hard and any girl with a big bust who can play that well is amazing." It gave Jayne a chance she didn't often get. Sylvia Herscher says, "She had great pretensions to musicality and intellectuality. At the drop of the hat out came the violin." Most people discouraged Jayne from displaying her musical skills, but she'd play and sing in her thin little voice whenever she had the chance. And some people, like Byron, admired her bravado. "She had guts. She always struck the first blow," he said.

That summer Jayne made a movie which Shiffrin calls the "key mistake." Jerry Wald at Fox wanted Jayne to play second to Suzy Parker in a Cary Grant film called *Kiss Them For Me*. It was another giggly blonde role. Wald knew Shiffrin was opposed to the idea. As a come-on Wald dangled a part in front of Jayne which she was desperate to have, the title role in a film about Jean Harlow. Jayne had been interested in Harlow's career for a long time. She was forever mentioning her. "Life is a big waterfall. I

○ ○ ○ ○ ○ ○ ○ ○ ○ ○ ○ ○ ○ ○ ○ ○ ○ ○ ○ ○ ○ ○ ○ ○ ○ ○ ○ ○ ○ ○ ○ ○ ○ ○ ○ ○ ○ ○

want to freeze at the top. Just like Jean Harlow did. Her life reminds me so much of that beautiful poem by Kelly and Sheats about the athlete who died young.''

Jayne and Shiffrin had several violent scenes about the Cary Grant movie. He said, ''I'm supposed to be handling your career. I wish you weren't the custodian of your career. I wish I could talk directly to your career. You shouldn't even consider the *Kiss Them* part.''

The next time they discussed it Bill remembers, ''I pulled a low-down trick. I never did it before and I've never done it since and it was the only way to prove to Jayne that she was going to be unmercifully screwed. I got a secretary to attach a tape machine to the phone and called Jerry Wald and did what I consider a totally despicable thing. Wald said she'd never get the Harlow part. 'She's terrible. I just want her for *Kiss Them For Me*.'

''I said, 'Jerry, I don't understand, the studio didn't want her for Harlow?'

'' 'No. Absolutely not. She's all wrong for it.'

''I got him to reveal everything.''

Jayne came over to Bill's office. He told her that Fox didn't want her for the Harlow role, only for *Kiss Them For Me*.

Jayne said, ''You're just mad at them.''

''No,'' said Bill, ''I'm not. I wanted to get a rubber gun and go to your house and say, 'I'm the guy that made you and if anyone's going to destroy you, I'm going to.' ''

''I wish you had. It would have been a gas.''

''I've done something worse.''

''Oh, come on. Don't start that old record again.''

''No, it's a tape. It's something confidential, if you can keep your mouth shut.'' Bill played it for her and she was stunned. She asked if he would go out for a minute and let her listen to it alone.

"I understood the pain, but it was the only way I could teach her that I was in her corner."

She made the picture in the end. There were a couple of reasons, one that she was essentially starry-eyed and couldn't believe her good fortune at being in a movie with Cary Grant. Wald claimed that some of his sophistication would rub off on Jayne. It didn't but it wasn't for lack of rubbing. She never got used to her own success and acted like a tourist on her own set. The other reason for doing the film was that she was too insecure to wait for good material. As a friend put it later, she would have made *Jungle Girl Goes to the Moon* rather than do nothing.

Part of the film was shot in the studio in Los Angeles, and Vera, who was visiting at the time, remembers getting up with Jayne at 5:00 A.M. and watching her rehearse a scene with Grant over and over until "I was too tired to stand up. We came home in a limousine and Jayne was crying, she was so tired. She said, 'Mamma, I have to do it.'"

The rest of the film was shot on location at the Fairmount Hotel in San Francisco. Barbara Malley, an extra, recalls, "We were doing night scenes and it was cold. Jayne was wearing, when she wasn't on camera, a coat with a big fur collar and inside, sitting on her boobs, snuggled in the fur was a Chihuahua. Jayne was exactly the same off camera as on. She was all sexy little girl and big boobs role, no matter what. She was extremely friendly and nice to everyone — the extras, the grips, the cameramen — and everyone seemed very fond of her. Whereas someone like Suzy Parker was a different person off screen and she wasn't anyone's favorite by any means. Jayne would prance around and coo to her dog looking down at those big knockers and everyone just thought it was a real kick. She was having a good time and so was everyone else."

Jayne made a quick trip to Dallas after the movie was completed. Vera was a little taken aback by Jayne's cheesecake extravaganzas but she bravely told reporters, "As long as Jaynie believes in her heart she did the right thing I'm all for it. But I still don't understand how she kept from freezing to death."

When Jayne came home, Vera recalls, "She could pin up her hair and be at home." The family would sit around eating hot dogs in the kitchen and Jayne would watch herself arriving in Dallas on the news.

That visit Vera was about to throw an old red velvet evening purse away. Jayne said, "Oh, Mama, don't throw it away," and took it back to California with her. Later Vera saw a photograph of Jayne in an ermine coat holding her bag. "It was like a knife through my heart."

Jayne was in close if cautious touch with her mother. Jayne always said, "Mama, you've got troubles of your own. I'll never bring you mine." And she never did. To that extent, neither really had a very good idea about what the other was about. Still there was a powerful bond between them which didn't depend on confidences shared or information exchanged. It was a primitive combination of love, respect, history, dislike, and power struggling. Vera tried alternately to love Jayne into submission and fight her. Jayne withdrew.

Jayne flew back from Dallas to organize a champagne party honoring her newly completed swimming pool. Mickey had been laboring for months, digging and pouring concrete, and the result was the honeymoon pool on Wanda Park Drive. At the bottom of the small, rectangular pool's deep end is a crude painting of Jayne wearing a pale blue bikini and a mass of yellow hair. She is being nibbled at by two fat purple fish. The result looks like the cover of a salacious science-fiction book. Jayne had an invitation printed in the Beverly Hills *Citizen* saying, "Hope you'll be tickled pink and accept my invitation for christening my pink swimming pool with pink champagne yet, Wednesday, September 18 at 4 P.M." Throngs of people showed up and Jayne posed in and about the pool with Mickey and the animals. The pool was filled with pink champagne.

Jayne was also celebrating her first trip to Europe. After shooting four films, Fox decided to send her on a promotional tour, a sort of It's-Tuesday-It-Must-be-Belgium package of sixteen countries in thirty days. It was an ur-Mansfield spectacle. She got mobbed in Italy by raucous fans who stole a thousand-dollar garter from her. Her manager, Bill Winter, saved her from further Italian enthusiasm by carrying her inside. It was the first of many progressively more violent episodes which excited Jayne and which she excited. She was also presented to the Queen of England, for whom she stuffed herself into a high-necked dress of champagne-colored silk jersey. Years before Monroe had caused disapproval by appearing at Buckingham Palace in extensive décolletage. The audience sniggered at Jayne's slit skirt and roared at her curtsy. "My first curtsy ever," Jayne said. Afterward Jayne remembered, "It was the most exciting moment of my life. I was never in awe of any woman before — but I was terribly in awe of her. Everything about her was so marvelous — from the first moment she came in and the band played 'My Country, 'Tis of Thee' . . . 'You are so beautiful, your majesty,' " said Jayne.

Elizabeth II returned the compliment. "The Queen," said Jayne, "has a great inner beauty. I looked at her the way I've seen my fans look at me. I was shivering with ecstasy."

The studio sent Jayne around the northeast when she returned from Europe. She had a private railroad car which whistle-stopped its way through New England and on

○ ○ ○ ○ ○ ○ ○ ○ ○ ○ ○ ○ ○ ○ ○ ○ ○ ○ ○ ○ ○ ○ ○ ○ ○ ○ ○ ○ ○ ○ ○ ○ ○ ○ ○ ○ ○

south to Washington.  At every stop along the way Jayne
would hand out autographed pictures and whisper thanks
to the crowd into a microphone.  The car cost Fox $685, not
including refreshments for reporters.  Jayne, dressed con-
servatively in a loose-fitting pink suit, said she was aban-
doning cheesecake.  "I'm making a switch from the kind of
clothes I've been wearing.  I have used cheesecake publicity to get my foot in the door.  I now have it very definitely
in the door.  From now on I want people to think of my
face and the roles I have done rather than my pinup pictures.  I feel there's so much cheesecake out on me that I
don't have to replenish the supply.  My fans know what I
have to offer physically.  I've decided that even if I have to
wear dresses up to here [pointing to her chin] I'll do it to
get people to notice my face.  I don't want to depend on
my wiggle.  It distracts from the polished comedy I would
like to project."

Jayne's publicity since returning to Hollywood bears
some scrutiny.  It was characterized by its inconsistency
and circumscribed by the boundaries of Jayne's active but
limited imagination.  Surprisingly, her major concern was
still getting her name spelled right.  To the dismay of the
studio, which provided her with dignified tours, she still
concentrated on making "everyone stop in their tracks."

Jayne had a five-year plan for establishing herself in the
affections of the whole country.  She outlined it to Richard
Donovan of *The Saturday Evening Post*.  "The first step,
which is to get all the men stirred up, is about three-
quarters completed, as I see it.  The next step — the one
I'm working on now — is to get all the women stirred up.
This could backfire.  To make it work I'll probably have to
start emphasizing home life and the PTA and all that.
When that's done, I may take a shot at the intellectuals."

Donovan mentioned an eastern pinup establishment

which was bootlegging revealing pictures of Jayne. He wondered if she would order an injunction. "Injunction? What do I want with an injunction? Send more pictures immediately! There may be somebody somewhere who doesn't have one! I don't care who they are — men, women, children, grandmothers! We were made for each other!"

Her plan was to be a top Hollywood star in two years and win an Academy Award in five. "I work hard and do my best and I always have this real high feeling, this racked up go, go, go. So I don't see why I shouldn't get what I want."

Donovan asked her about a New York reporter's story of finding her nude in a bathtub splashing around while a slew of fans took pictures. "Man," said Jayne, "that was a turkey shoot."

Jayne gave advice to others who wanted to follow along her path. "To establish yourself as an actress, you have to become well known. A girl just starting out, I would tell her to concentrate on acting, but she doesn't," said Jayne in an unparalleled understatement, "have to go around wearing blankets."

"Some little girls get lost in Hollywood, but they would have been lost in their hometowns, or anywhere else. You have to be noticed by the right people to get ahead in Hollywood and you can't afford to be noticed with the wrong people." Jayne may have believed this but she certainly didn't act upon it. She hung around almost exclusively with the wrong people, starting with Mickey. A story her third husband, Matt Cimber, tells illustrates how egalitarian she was. Darryl Zanuck invited Jayne to an intimate dinner party and Jayne brought the uninvited Mickey along. Zanuck took her aside and asked why she'd brought him. "Oh," she said airily, "I thought Mrs. Zanuck might be lonely." As Cimber put it, "If she didn't dig you she wouldn't have anything to do with you. And if she did, you could be a bus boy and you'd score."

In a moment of reflection about the nature of publicity Jayne said, "If you've got nothing but publicity you might as well go back to Texas. But if you have acting ability and films to back up the publicity, that's it — you've got it made. Publicity has always come to me. I haven't gone to it. But I've been cooperative. It's better to have the press on your side."

In her endeavors to cooperate with the press Jayne developed some athletic routines with Mickey. He customarily flung her around at the beach. In their favorite act, the bird, Jayne, balanced on Mickey's palm and made like a swan. Byron suggested Mickey and Jayne enter the Press Photographers Ball doing their bird. Mickey said, well gee, he didn't really know, but Jayne was all fired up and insisted. Mickey was willing to go along because he loved Jayne and wanted to be at the center of her attention. Since her attention was centered on herself, he had to be so close to her that when she looked at herself she saw him too.

In a variation of the bird, Jayne and Mickey got themselves matching leopard-skin bikinis and he pressed her, carrying her around the Ballyhoo Ball of the Screen Publicists Association in October 1957. Reporter Dick Williams said, "It was obvious that Jayne Mansfield's rugged New York picture-grabbing training stood her in good stead. Giving ground to no adversary, whether she be Mamie Van Doren (in black tights and hip-length black mesh hose) or Barbara Nichols (in sheer negligee), Jayne (in leopard-skin bikini) was carried around on the brawny hands of her muscleman, Mickey Hargitay."

Jayne's notices were not always moderate. Louella Parsons asked her the following unwieldy rhetorical question:

○ ○ ○ ○ ○ ○ ○ ○ ○ ○ ○ ○ ○ ○ ○ ○ ○ ○ ○ ○ ○ ○ ○ ○ ○ ○ ○ ○ ○ ○ ○ ○ ○ ○ ○ ○ ○

"Why did you let Mickey Hargitay take you in his arms and hold you up to the last row of bleachers so you could sign autographs at a recent Hollywood première?"

Another of Jayne's cooperative efforts took place at the Crown Room at a party to launch Sophia Loren's American career. Jim Byron and Jayne arrived to see Loren stepping out of her car. Jayne said, "Let's go around the block again to make a later entrance."

Jayne managed to get seated next to Loren and, as Jim puts it, "She began pulling and pulling at her dress." It couldn't hold up under such pulling since the dress was cut exactly at nipple line. Finally Jayne got exasperated, stood up, plucked one breast out of the dress and leaned over Sophia with a wide crocodile smile. There is a series of wonderful pictures from the event. First Loren looks disapprovingly down Jayne's bosom. Then Jayne, smiling broadly, stands over the doubtful Loren. And finally there is the photograph UPI man Ernie Schwark took of Jayne, smiling dazzlingly with one of her breasts exposed.

Jayne tried to placate Louella Parsons. "I am normally a very quiet home-loving girl and really shy," she told Parsons. "I would much rather stay quietly at home with my little daughter, Jaynie, and have a dinner before a fireplace, but when I came to Hollywood I was told you have to go to all the previews, premières and happenings. I know now that I must pick and choose the places I go and I must not wear dresses too low or try to attract too much attention.

"I can't say I blame some of the newspaper people for saying it was too low, because when I bent over Sophia Loren too much of me was exposed. I saw it in the photographs and I was shocked myself."

Loren said, "I would never wear a dress like that."

Jayne, throwing caution, Parsons and Hopper to the winds said, "Maybe she can't afford to wear dresses like this. You know if you wave a flag it has to have something to hold it up. It doesn't just stay up by itself." The meta-phor is a little tortured, and Jayne's flag didn't stay up very long, but publicity had come to her.

The results of the unrelenting publicity focused on such an unfocused subject as Jayne's personality were confound-ing. Because it was news when she opened her mouth, it followed that she had to talk, frequently when she had nothing to say, to be news. Her remarks ranged from serious to contradictory, to funny, to inane, to idiosyn-cratic. Almost daily she revealed to the press her own con-fusion about who she was and what she was doing.

"My kind of girl," she announced, "has finally come into her own. The ideal of the good, old-fashioned, earthy but elegant American beauty is now launched as the leading 'fashion.' It's the look of the big saucy eyes, the full rich red lips, the cheeks softly rouged. Any woman can have it, if she knows her way around make-up, and will take the time to do it right by herself." If any woman could have it then there was nothing special about Jayne.

But Jayne had other qualifications. "Sex is very big this year and I am glad that I am too. If I didn't have a large bosom, people would talk about my small one. So what's the difference? I'm glad I have a large one." A public rela-tions man from Borden's asked her what she thought her greatest attributes were. "Why, you're from Borden's. You ought to know what my attributes are. In a way they're the same as Elsie's. I know Elsie very well, she's always upstaging me."

Then she had doubts. "It seems to me that men's inter-est is shifting. For the past five years they have been more interested in the anterior than in the posterior, if you know what I mean. But I think that's all going out of style." Jayne didn't think for a minute that interest in her pair was diminishing and made the remark because she liked the coy euphemisms. But she gave her body a lot of thought and attention. She treated it like a valuable antique. She dieted, sun-tanned, oiled and painted it with deliberation and impersonality. She became a commodity to herself.

All actresses, dancers, singers and models have to take care of their physical properties, and all of them become, to some degree, separated from themselves by highly critical narcissism. The face, voice or body becomes objectified. In Jayne's case the purpose of objectification was sexual attraction, which made her experience common to most women and different from that of a singer, for example. Jayne had an exaggerated form of women's anxiety about being desirable.

Jayne talked about herself as if she were an item in a department store. She declared that she was a star. "They talk about a different picture for me every day and everybody calls me Miss Mansfield, not Jayne. Right now they've got six pictures lined up for me after I finish this one, and they're exploiting me properly too. I was never exploited properly by Hollywood before, but now I've got six sittings for the movie magazine covers this week — a field I've never exploited before." In 1957 "exploit" still applied to natural resources.

Jayne had rules for her own behavior. "I don't believe in this new fad of blue jeans and sweaters worn by some actresses and I wouldn't allow myself to be seen on the streets with my hair up and no make-up as one blond actress did so out in Beverly Hills." She found this behavior subversively unstarlike, preferring to do her marketing in a tan, a small bikini and two Chihuahuas.

Jayne's basic confusion stemmed from the fact that society told her she had to have it two ways. She had to be simultaneously sexy and innocent. Jayne defined the "It" in *The Girl Can't Help It:* "It's sex appeal, what else. This girl I play has the most fabulous body in the world, but she's unaware of her sex appeal. All she wants to be is a wife and mother, but sex keeps getting in the way. She's like me, you might say . . . It's a perfect part for me because I understand the girl so well. She's like me, you know, the personality of a June Allyson with a fabulous figure.

"I am completely unaware of my sex appeal although others are aware of it. I'm glad it's that way. I didn't want to start out on the Mae West basis."

Jayne defined sex appeal variously: "It's just knowing what to do and then doing it with a lot of naiveté. Well, I shall be more specific. If a girl has curviness, exciting lips and a certain breathlessness, it helps. And it won't do a bit of harm if she has a kittenish, soft cuddly quality."

She also said, "Men want women to be pink, helpless and do a lot of deep breathing." And she concluded later, "It's what you have inside. The rest is all tinsel. Sex appeal has nothing to do with bodily proportions."

Jayne's pretend innocence derived from her infatuation with Shirley Temple and only created prurience. As Jayne learned it, sexually knowledgeable women were whores. What she couldn't incorporate was that little-girl women made men into child molesters.

Jayne thought sex was a very volatile issue. She told Mike Wallace: "I think movies have to be censored. Otherwise your child's mind will be corrupted. What they hear on the screen they will do in their private lives and you would have a lot of very unhappy results. Without censorship, you would whet the appetites of the nation to a point that could be entirely destructive to the world."

Sex, to Jayne, was like a dangerous explosive. It frightened her, but she felt she could handle it. Her children had to be protected, however. When she later made movies she didn't want them to see, they had to be protected from her as well. She thought the volatile component of sex demanded repression. She must have thought repressive measures would protect her, too, from her worst in-

stincts. Again and again you can hear the wrenching ambivalence, niggling with words, covering herself with
handfuls of euphemisms.

Wallace said, "Jayne, *you* certainly can't knock sex too
much . . . It's done a great deal for you."

"Mike, my career has been built on *womanliness*, not
sex!"

"What's the difference?"

"One is a ruder word than the other. I think 'sex' can
have so many distasteful connotations whereas 'womanliness' means something purer and sweeter." Jayne was on
the right track in attempting to distinguish "woman" from
"sex," but she got derailed in trying to make a case for
sweetness and light. She plunged on defensively. "We
have lots of sides to us. One of my sides happens to be
that I have a certain obvious femininity that others have
chosen to exploit . . ." She was forced to look for an escape hatch, an alibi, a patsy. Someone had to take the
blame for her sexuality.

Sometimes she was semifrank. "With a figure like mine
a girl is certain to attract attention, and I find it pleasing
and necessary that men look at me." "Necessary" is the
operative word describing the Jayne who couldn't survive
without her dose of wolf whistles.

Sometimes she was crafty. "When men get too attentive
I give them the Mansfield Routine. I tell them how much I
trust them and value their advice and friendship. This
startles the wolfiest of wolves into submission and almost
immediately he becomes fatherly, or even brotherly."

Other times she was discouraged and even afraid of her
own powers. "I have never met a man who didn't make a
pass at me. They start by wanting to be my friend. The
old ones are worse than the young ones. We talk a while
and sooner or later I find that they are not listening to me.
They just keep staring and moving closer."

Jim Bishop commented, "Still she is shrewd enough to know that the day men stop making passes at her, Jayne Mansfield is through." No one allowed her to voice the smallest complaint about the trap she was in, her distrust or her fear. Jim Byron said, admiringly, "No man ever controlled her." He failed to understand that all men did, which was a terminal, not a temporary condition.

At the end of her New England tour Jayne told Alfred Bester of *Holiday* magazine, "The publicity I'm used to is not me inside. I want to project the real me. There is more than one, two or three dimensions to me. All my life I've wanted to be an actress. I've exploited myself, but now I don't need it. Now that people know the name, I'm changing the policy. People know me but don't know who I am."

After the tour, Jayne went to a première in Hollywood with Jim Bishop. He described her as "serious and worried. She saw the fans behind sawhorses, she told the driver to pull close to the curb and slow down. She threw off the white mink, wriggled the shoulder straps lower, exposed her bosom, leaned across me and smiled as the idiots aimed their cameras into the window."

# *Memories Are Made of This*

♥ ♥ ♥

WHEN JAYNE arrived home in early November 1957, Mickey greeted her with an engagement ring. Mickey shied away from making the presentation in front of reporters because he was afraid "it would look like a cheap publicity stunt." Instead he gave Jayne the ring in the car on the way from the airport and the couple called a press conference when they got home. Jayne said, "It's the great moment of my life. I didn't think anything could top that experience [meeting the Queen] but this even surpasses that great thrill. All I ever wanted was a simple band of gold." Jayne was speaking metaphorically since, in Mickey's name, she had stood herself to a ten-carat diamond. She went on, "I want it to be a small wedding. I think marriage is a sacred thing. I don't want a lot of publicity."

Jayne had been deliberating about marriage for a long time. The previous November she told Hedda Hopper ". . . I'm not divorced from my husband. Mickey is in the process of being divorced. I'll devote myself to work during this seven-year contract. That takes me to thirty. After that I can have four kids. You see I'm in good shape."

o o o o o o o o o o o o o o o o o o o o o o o o o o o o o o o o o o o

"Take my situation — my baby Jayne Marie is almost six and I'm getting her routined in school. I give my evenings to her. After work I go home, have a fat steak, cream my face and then go to bed. I have to be up at five A.M. and at the studio by six. How does a husband fit into that schedule?"

Then again, Jayne said, "Mickey just turned down a picture with Hedy Lamarr. He can see nobody but me and vice versa. He has the same problem I have — the outer body is deceiving."

Mickey concurred about their similar problems in body English: "Like Jayne I try to keep my waist down and my chest up."

In early 1957 she was saying, "Too many Hollywood stars are getting married too fast. First they're glamorous girls, then they're engaged and married, and suddenly all the glamour fades. It then becomes a matter of household and babies at a time when they should be free to exploit themselves and the pictures they're making."

On the other hand, she said, "Mickey is not only powerful and gentle, but he's deep. He wants my career for me even more than I do. I wish all girls could be movie stars and that all men could look like Mickey."

In July Jayne explained the preconditions for her marriage. "First, Mickey's going to build us a heart-shaped house with a heart-shaped pool in Bel Air. Mickey has everything every woman has dreamed of . . . it's amazing he has so much. We will build this fantastic house and have all our dreams come true. We both want our careers to boom and together we will reach the tippy-top of the highest mountain."

Heady stuff. Over the months Mickey had been incorporated into the Mansfield road show, of which the wedding was to be the climax. The teeth of Jayne's imagination had bitten firmly into the idea of marriage. She

couldn't resist the spectacle. It was the scene at the end of
the movie: boy weds girl in a pink riot of bliss. Besides,
boy "has the greatest pectorals west of the Mississippi.
Possibly the world."

The studio hoped Jayne would stay single to enhance her
romantic allure, but she wouldn't do without Mickey. As a
romantic it was impossible for her to allow her relationship
with Mickey to remain in limbo. It had to be taken to its
logical conclusion. She waited until after her European
tour when there was a lull in activity. She looked forward
to their married life as a continual festival of romance and
publicity.

Jayne percolated with ideas for the wedding. "I may get
married in a white satin bikini bathing suit down at the
beach. My husband could wear one too. It could be a fabulous marriage. We'd have everybody from all over the
world. I've thought about it for a year now. We could use
that little glass church at Palos Verdes. We'd have everybody in bathing suits for the reception. All out in the
warm sun. No quiet little ceremony in Connecticut for
me." Although she lost out on the bathing suits, Jayne
won her glass church.

After their engagement was announced, Jayne and
Mickey took off with Bob Hope on his Christmas USO
tour. They entertained in Hawaii, Korea, Guam and
Japan. In Tokyo Jayne split her kimono. In Honolulu,
Hope said, "I heard the biggest roar in show business
when Jayne came on."

When the couple returned from the Far East they just had
time to get ready for the January 13, 1958, wedding.
Mickey and Jayne invited one hundred of their closest
friends, of whom fifty were newsmen. The invitations
were naturally pink, instructing guests to report to the
Wayfarers' Chapel in Palos Verdes Estates at 8:00 P.M. The
chapel is on a high cliff south of Los Angeles overlooking

o o o o o o o o o o o o o o o o o o o o o o o o o o o o o o o o o o o

Portuguese Bend and the Pacific. Frank Lloyd Wright designed the nondenominational church as a monument to Emanuel Swedenborg. It is fundamentally a glass A-frame. Jayne was pleased that the Wayfarers' Chapel afforded the congregation a view of the ocean and outsiders a view of the congregation.

The Reverend Kenneth W. Knox who officiated was nervous about the dignity of his church, but Jayne and Mickey reassured him that theirs was to be a quiet, simple affair. Knox stressed the fact that there were to be no cameras.

Harry Brand at Fox handed the public relations aspect of the wedding over to Jim Byron. "It was the most spectacular wedding ever," said Jim. "There was never anything like it. It was headlines for one week before the wedding." Byron and Jayne kept the event on the front page for longer than one could have thought possible. Jayne's wardrobe, her thoughts on Mickey, children, religion, love, sex and womanhood enthralled readers every morning. "I don't need a bikini now," said Jayne, explaining that as a married woman she no longer felt it appropriate to look sexy.

Jayne said she intended to get rid of the dozens of laminated magazine covers on which she had appeared. They decorated the Wanda Park Drive house and subsequently covered the walls of Mickey and Jayne's pink palace. "When we move I'll probably just take them down and stuff them in the cellar." She never did take them off display and Mickey still has them.

"You know," she said the next day, "there might be something to that mother stuff. I think a man wants to be mothered by the woman he loves. He wants to feel that she is protecting him. Mickey feels I am like his mother." Jayne had a breezy way of zeroing in on the fantasies and complexities of male-female behavior. She understood the threat women posed men and how that threat was de-

The essential Jayne Mansfield, in one of eleven bathrooms
at the pink palace. *Wide World*

*Top:* Three-year-old Jayne in Phillipsburg, New Jersey. *Harry and Vera Peers*

*Bottom:* Harry and Vera Peers with Paul Mansfield, Dallas, 1951. *Harry and Vera Peers*

*Top:* Jayne and Vera Peers, Dallas, 1946. *Harry and Vera Peers*

*Bottom:* Jayne and matching Jayne Marie, Beverly Hills, 1954. *Harry and Vera Peers*

*Top:* Jayne and Tony Randall in subtle pas de deux in *Will Success Spoil Rock Hunter?*

Jayne at the champagne hour.

Jayne's early love of animals never faltered. *Anchorage Times*

Jayne and Harry Peers before her marriage to Mickey at Portuguese Bend, California. *Wide World*

Jayne and Mickey at the Peerses' wedding reception in Dallas.
*Harry and Vera Peers*

Jayne and Mickey arrive in
Paris, 1959. *Wide World*

The arms belong to Mickey.
*Eric Skipsey*

An American family. *Harry and Vera Peers*

Mickey, Mickey, Jr., Jayne
and Jayne Marie in front of
Mickey's homemade
avalanche at the pink palace.
*Harry and Vera Peers*

Vera at the piano in the pink palace, with Jayne Marie, Jayne and the
Mickeys. *Harry and Vera Peers*

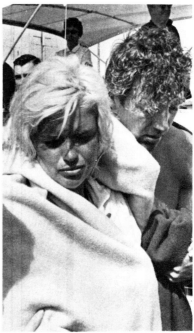

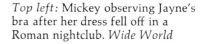

*Top left:* Mickey observing Jayne's bra after her dress fell off in a Roman nightclub. *Wide World*

*Top right:* Jayne and Mickey after their unexpected night on Rose Island in the Bahamas. *Wide World*

Monks experiencing a crisis of faith in Bangkok. *Wide World*

Matt Cimber and Jayne demonstrating the twist at a New
York discotheque, 1965. *Wide World*

Christmas 1966: Jayne welcomes Zoltan home from the hospital after his mauling by a lion. *Wide World*

Jayne completed her last movie, *Single Room Furnished*, two weeks before she died. *Wide World*

Sam Brody and Jayne going into Parliament,
London, 1967. *Wide World*

*Top:* The car in which Jayne died, June 1967. *Wide World*

*Bottom:* Harry Peers and a gaunt Mickey comfort Vera
Peers at Jayne's funeral, Pen Argyl, Pennsylvania.
*Wide World*

flected by turning sexually active women into mothers. Sanctified, they no longer frightened child-men.

Jayne was prepared to protect and mother Mickey for her own sake as well as his. She was under the impression that Mickey and marriage were going to change her. She was counting on him and the institution to curtail her own sexuality, to protect her from the excesses of her exhibitionism and the consequences of her eroticism. What she didn't take into account was that Mickey's passive acceptance of her accounted for their excellent relations. Any attempt at remodeling her and they started fighting.

"I do want everything to be dignified," Jayne said. "We're very serious about this marriage. We don't want a lot of publicity." On the evening of the event there was a group of what Bill Shiffrin called "five thousand goons" lined up on the highway above the chapel waiting to see the bride and groom. Jim Byron estimated 30,000, but crowd estimates are notoriously difficult for a press agent. Jayne emerged from her limousine late. She was wearing a pale pink lace dress designed for a smaller woman. The gown was skin-tight to the knee, then flaired in two tiers of flounces. Ross Christena was Mickey's best man. Columnist May Mann was maid of honor. Jayne said, "I wanted to make Jaynie Marie my flower girl, but I didn't think it would be right for a second marriage." Jayne hobbled down the aisle while Donald Maloof sang "Because." At the altar, she met Mickey done up in an Italian silk mohair tuxedo with swirls of purple and black. Someone had taken away his white socks and given him black ones to go with his patent leather pumps. Bob Hope was sitting in the front row making faces at Jayne. Someone leaned over to Shiffrin during the proceedings and said, "Don't worry, you're not losing a client, you're gaining an adviser."

Halfway through the ceremony the spectators outside

went berserk. The highway patrolmen threw up their hands in despair as the fans lobbed tomatoes, fruit and even rocks at the chapel. The photographers, of whom Byron says there were five hundred, began taking pictures though the glass, and hundreds of flash bulbs dazzled the congregation. The crowd started shouting, "We want Jayne. We want Mickey." Fortunately weddings don't last very long, six minutes in this case, and Jayne and Mickey were able to greet their public before the church was razed. As Byron was shepherding the couple to the car he saw policemen trying to move the crowd back up the hill to the highway. One stout lady couldn't make it back up and slipped down, squashing an officer.

Finally the three made it to the car and Byron started to drive away, very slowly because there were fans all over the hood. Two hands reached in to pull Byron out the window when a voice said, "That isn't Mickey, let him go." They got lost on the way to the airport and were stopped for speeding. Instead of a ticket they got a police escort to the airport. They had missed their flight to Dallas but got one early the next morning.

Vera and Harry had put together a local reception for the Hargitays. Jayne was wearing a singularly unflattering cocktail dress of electric pink satin. Her spike heels were dyed-to-match. She greeted guests, cut an extraordinary cake and drank champagne out of her electric pink shoe. She even scrambled some eggs for Mickey to demonstrate her domesticity. Vera looks at pictures of Jayne gazing adoringly at Mickey, shakes her head sadly and says, "She was so happy." The next day Jayne and Mickey took off for the Eden Roc Hotel in Miami Beach where they spent their honeymoon with Ross Christena. As he recalls, "Miami Beach rolled out the rug for her. There were plans to name a street after her." It turned out to be an alley behind the 23rd street fire station. Jayne, Mickey

and Ross promoted themselves a delirious honeymoon of
free food, free drinks and free publicity.

Right after the honeymoon, Jayne and Mickey went to
Las Vegas for a six-week stint at the Tropicana. Their act
consisted of Jayne moving around in a long, tight net dress
scattered with sequins designed to cover nipples and pubic
hair. "It has elegance, charm and dignity," she said.
When Jayne moved, the sequins moved too, away from
their planned locations. She said, "I designed it myself. I
wanted to be completely covered. If I had tried to compete
with the nudes on their own grounds, it would have been
bad taste. And besides those girls are not as healthy as I.
They have been through a war and all that hardship."
Jayne had a male chorus behind her who watched her bug-
eyed and sang or moaned. Mickey contributed his adagio
dance skills. He picked Jayne up and threw her around in
various attitudes of abandon. Jayne made twenty thousand a week and Mickey made five. The rest of the time
Jayne and Mickey sat around the pool signing autographs,
taking the sun and playing with the dogs they had brought
along.

Late that winter Jayne, Mickey and Jayne Marie left for
Europe. Jayne was starring in a movie called *The Sheriff of
Fractured Jaw*. Mickey observed, "No one can deny that
Jaynie has a fabulous figure. She can act too. In this new
picture . . . she rides a horse and shoots a gun."

Jayne said, "It's fabulous. It's got cowboys and Indians
and everything. It's a British Western shot in Spain. I
play a completely different type of girl. She's a definite
character opposite to the roles I've been playing. This girl
runs the town while she runs a saloon."

The film concerns an Englishman who comes to the Wild
West to sell guns. He is a tenderfoot but manages to bluff
his way through a lot of tough situations with gunslingers,
Indians and range warriors. His exploits endear him to the

o o o o o o o o o o o o o o o o o o o o o o o o o o o o o o o o o o o o o o o

capacious heart of Jayne/Kate, owner of the local saloon.
Jayne plays the role with a lot of gusto and an imperfectly
thought-out accent which falls somewhere between Fort
Laramie and Newark.  The most remarkable feature of the
production is Jayne's corseting which allowed her, three
months pregnant, to squeeze into incredibly wasp-waisted
costumes.

In July a European reporter asked her to raise her skirt a
trifle for a photograph.  Jayne refused.  "I am going to be a
mother sometime between December third and December
ninth so I don't think this is the time for it.  Expecting
mothers shouldn't.

"The baby is due in December, but I don't care whether
it's a boy or a girl so long as it looks like Mickey.  If it's a
boy we'll name him Miklos, after Mickey.  If it's a girl
she'll be Camille Yvonne.  I once played a character named
Camille in a movie.

"I won't be making any appearances on TV until next
year — after the baby.  Somehow it doesn't seem right for
a girl in my condition to be working in front of an audience.  Everybody would be worrying about me instead of
enjoying the show, if you know what I mean.

"Sack dresses have saved me from buying maternity
clothes.  I've bought more than twenty sacks, and no one
can tell I'm expecting.  Every girl in the country could be
pregnant, but with the new styles who can tell?

"Women are much more radiant and happy when they're
expecting.  After this one arrives we plan to have others.
Gosh knows, we certainly have enough bedrooms in the
house for a large family."

The house Jayne mentioned was a stucco affair in
Holmby Hills, next to Bel Air.  It had been built in 1929 by
a Texas oil man.  He sold it in the thirties to Rudy Vallee
from whom Jayne and Mickey bought it for $76,000.  It had
eight bedrooms and, Jayne was fond of pointing out, thir-

o o o o o o o o o o o o o o o o o o o o o o o o o o o o o o o o o o o o

teen bathrooms.  It's a three-story Spanish-style house, set
back from Sunset Boulevard behind a high stone and
stucco fence.  The grounds are large and landscaped with
tropical extravagance.  Jayne and Mickey decorated it with
a quantity of grillwork, including a huge iron gate which
had J and M entwined in a grillwork heart.  When they
bought the house Jayne gave out that Mickey had presented it to her on the occasion of their marriage.  The
money, in fact, came from Jayne's grandfather's estate and
the sale of the Wanda Park Drive house.

This announcement raised some questions with the
ex–Mrs. Hargitay about where Mickey had been hiding his
wealth all the while.  Mary Birge Hargitay's lawyer said,
"If at the time of their divorce Mickey had $2000, nobody
knew where it was."  Mickey was paying $20 a week to
support his daughter, Tina.  Mary initiated proceedings
that fall to raise the payments to $415.

Mickey and Jayne came back from Europe full of their
trip.  Spain, said Jayne, was "very quaint.  The people
over there are so Spanish."  About the English she said,
"They aren't as reserved as people think.  Even English-
men behave like men when the right girl is around."  But
she thought she wouldn't go back.  "Never again.  You
can't get a decent hamburger or malted over there.  It's
nice in some little cultural ways.  But they don't even have
barbecues in their back yards.  And that's what I missed
most of all."  Mickey set about installing a barbecue in
their back yard, but the child support case hampered his
progress.

After creating a bogus fortune for Mickey out of some
fictitious real estate deals he was to have transacted in Indianapolis, Jayne and Mickey had to retrench and poor-
mouth.  Jayne admitted Mickey's fortune had been cooked
up for its romantic value.  Life at the pink palace, they
implied, wasn't much better than living through the siege

○ ○ ○ ○ ○ ○ ○ ○ ○ ○ ○ ○ ○ ○ ○ ○ ○ ○ ○ ○ ○ ○ ○ ○ ○ ○ ○ ○ ○ ○ ○ ○ ○ ○ ○ ○ ○ ○

of Leningrad.  They slept on a foam mattress on the floor. They sat on two rattan chairs, staring desolately at the sole decoration, Mickey's barbells.  "Even the two servants sleep on the floor, on mattresses like us, you understand," said Mickey.  "We could afford to buy furniture," he went on, "but we don't have time to shop and buy exactly what we want — and we can't afford to make any mistakes."  As it turned out, every article which was to grace the palace was promoted, so the Hargitays never did risk an error in judgment.

The desperation of Jayne and Mickey's financial situation prompted Laguna Beach police lieutenant John S. Zelko, Jr., to circulate a memo to his fellow policemen.  "Attention all officers: Please be advised that we shall each donate $10 from our next paycheck to Jayne Mansfield for the purchase of bedroom furniture.  Each officer may give more if he so desires."

Meanwhile, Mickey had to give the court an accounting of his resources.  He reported making $125 a week as Jayne's personal manager, although other sources say $500. He said he had about $10,000 in cash when he married. He was still paying for a 1955 Cadillac.  He owed $3000 on the diamond he had given Jayne.  He was paying $1500 a month on the pink palace.  He had made $56,000 in Las Vegas, including his salary and his manager's cut.

Jerome Lipsky handled Mickey's case.  Greg Bautzer had bowed out of Jayne's affairs.  He told her he was a corporation lawyer.  "Well," she said, "I'm a corporation."  But Bautzer wasn't persuaded.  He said, "She listened mostly to Mickey.  You can't compete with pillow talk.  Take a big strong man with the pillow and he's stronger than Henry Kissinger or the CIA.  I referred her to another lawyer."

Lipsky felt that Mary Hargitay was trying to fleece Jayne and Mickey because they were Hollywood celebrities.

○ ○ ○ ○ ○ ○ ○ ○ ○ ○ ○ ○ ○ ○ ○ ○ ○ ○ ○ ○ ○ ○ ○ ○ ○ ○ ○ ○ ○ ○ ○ ○ ○ ○ ○ ○ ○ ○ ○ ○

"Mrs. Hargitay wanted five thousand dollars a month or something. She thought Mickey was getting ten percent of Jayne's earnings and could afford it. In truth he was getting some for tax purposes and ego, but it was all part of the community property."

Jayne said that she and Mickey spent seventy-one dollars a month on Jaynie Marie and she couldn't understand why Tina Hargitay needed more. "I consider that love is the most important thing you can give a child. We spend about forty-five to fifty dollars a month on food and fifteen dollars a month on her clothing. This also includes two dental and two physical checkups a year."

Mary Hargitay said Tina needed dancing, ballet and swimming lessons as well as access to a heated pool. About the plea of no furniture she said, "It could be just a publicity stunt. They may have their furniture stashed away or something. I don't think they're as broke as all that."

Mary discussed her divorce from Mickey. He had, she said, promised to support Tina if Mary would give him a quiet divorce and not mention Jayne Mansfield. "I couldn't say at any time he had a desire to divorce me and to marry Miss Mansfield. He said he wanted to continue in show business and that she had made rather a lot of promises which he represented to me." He allegedly wanted the divorce so he could be seen around with Jayne, "who would make a motion picture star out of him."

"I have no objection to Mickey's seeing Tina. But I don't want that woman around. She stands for things I just don't believe in. She'd be a bad influence on my girl."

Mrs. Hargitay, who owned a three-foot bronze statue of Mickey in addition to his Mr. Universe Trophy, said, "I think that Mickey has gone off his rocker. As a matter of fact, he's aged terribly since I last saw him. He looks at

o o o o o o o o o o o o o o o o o o o o o o o o o o o o o o o o o o o o o

least fifteen years older than he did in nineteen fifty-six. He just keeps trailing that woman, fawning all over her. He's not the same Mickey Hargitay I married."

Love had transformed, if not informed Mickey Hargitay. In an imperceptive, not to mention inaccurate locution, he responded, "My most precious possession in the world is my wife, Jayne."

Mickey's devotion didn't impress Superior Court Commissioner John P. Oliver. "It's a sad commentary," he ruled on September 26, 1958, "that in the time this man has had $69,000 pass through his hands he has paid $800 for his child and hasn't even seen her since December of 1956. He is more interested in his own pursuits than in his own flesh and blood."

A newsman noted, "Throughout the day the muscleman ignored the presence of his daughter who had been taken to court to testify but was excused." Mickey explained that he did not wish to "confuse her. It would not be fair to interrupt her nine-year-old-mind with things she would never understand." Jayne filled in for him. "I feel that publicity is all right for people who can deal with it. But any kind of public sensationalism is bad for a little girl like this. We just wanted to make sure she got everything she wanted."

The judge told Mickey to pay $300 a month toward Tina's support. The Hargitays said, "We're very happy that this is all over and everyone can get back to normal." Lipsky said the case could "obviously" have been settled out of court, "But we were not going to let motion picture people be subjected to 'grabs' by anyone who came along."

In thanks for saving them $115 a month Jayne and Mickey gave Lipsky a gold money clip which he still carries. It has an Oscar on one side and the inscription reads, "For an outstanding performance, Love Jayne and Mickey." Lipsky says he used to show it around, covering up Mickey's name. "It was quite a conversation piece," he said, smirking.

With the case out of the way Jayne and Mickey could apply themselves to furnishing their home. Jayne predicted that "It's going to cost as much as we paid for the house and more. But it's our dream house and we expect to spend the rest of our lives there." It didn't turn out to be as expensive as Jayne thought.

Jim Byron was hard at work promoting furniture and building materials. He sent over fifteen hundred letters to various manufacturers describing the publicity possibilities of the palace. As he puts it, "I conned General Concrete into supplying the rocks for the pool and stone for the fence." Byron promised everyone that the house would be another Crystal Palace, that hundreds of thousands of people would be taken on tours to see, for example, General Concrete's rocks. One of Byron's letters fell into the hands of a hostile columnist who reprinted it to chastise press agents. Byron was perturbed until hundreds of offers for free merchandise started flooding in. Jim estimates that overall he promoted about $150,000 in goods for the palace.

Jayne continued to prove herself as a promoter. One afternoon she was walking down a street in Santa Monica when she passed a store with an $800 Lucite chair in the window. She told the proprietor that she would sit in his window and sign autographs for an afternoon if he would give her the chair. The owner got a lot of business and Jayne got a chair for her bathroom.

Not long afterward she was on the Mike Douglas Show in Philadelphia. She was appearing with Gypsy Rose Lee and a gentleman who built $15,000 garbage-disposal units. He offered one to Gypsy Rose, and Jayne, unable to keep still, announced that she lived in Beverly Hills and could use one too. The garbage-disposal man was somewhat taken aback but obliged Jayne with a unit. It remained un-

o o o o o o o o o o o o o o o o o o o o o o o o o o o o o o o o o o o o o

packed in the garage along with a lifetime supply of Firestone whitewalls and other assorted items which Jayne ferreted away. She was an incorrigible packrat, living out in heroic style the instincts of a mad lady with overflowing shopping bags.

Much of the house was furnished because the goods were free. Other items were selected with fastidiousness. Byron promoted some fluffy pink carpeting which was used on the floor and ceiling of the entryway and living room. Guests were required to take their shoes off upon entering the house. The living room contained a purple sofa, white and gold piano, religious statuary and several pictures of Jayne. High up on the orchid walls Mickey had stuck odd pieces of grillwork.

Glenn Holse, who designed Jayne's Las Vegas appearances, drew a mural for Jaynie Marie's room which featured Jayne as a witch in a peaked hat and Mickey as a friendly woodsman. There was a squirrel with a heart-shaped bellybutton, trees with heart-shaped leaves and candy-cane branches and a musical bus. Jaynie Marie had a miniature grand piano.

Just before Christmas Jayne was ready to deliver her baby. Vera and Harry sped across Texas, Arizona and New Mexico, picking up speeding tickets along the way, in order to get to Jayne before the baby was born. When they pulled up, Jayne was waiting in a red, accordion-pleated chiffon robe. "I couldn't go to the hospital until you arrived," she said. Mickey then brought around one Cadillac, but Jayne turned it down and selected another for her hospital entrance. Miklos was born at St. John's Hospital in Santa Monica at 5:00 A.M., December 21, 1958. He was a week late and completely healthy, weighing 9 lbs. 9½ oz. Jayne was, in Vera's word, "radiant." She loved small creatures and had a very special talent for socializing with infants and small animals. She could be completely affectionate with them and they loved her back completely. Mickey, Jr., was a great joy to her.

Jayne bought Mickey an I.D. bracelet saying "chained to you forever" and a watch saying "Till the end of time." Mickey bought Jayne a miniature music box saying "you are always in tune" and a charm bracelet inscribed, "Begun, January 13, 1958, End — never." Jayne called Mickey "Peachy." He called her "Oochy."

Mickey summed up his thoughts about the year. "When I hear people say that America is the land of opportunity I say 'Wow.' Where else could a crazy Hungarian get wealthy and Jayne Mansfield too?" Where indeed?

# *Personality*

♥ ♥ ♥

*The Girl.* I rage at my own image in the glass
That's so unlike myself that when you praise it
It is as though you praised another, or even
Mocked me with praise of my mere opposite;
And when I wake towards morn I dread myself,
For the heart cries that what deception wins
Cruelty must keep; therefore be warned and go
If you have seen that image and not the woman.

"The Hero, The Girl, and the Fool"
W. B. YEATS

NINETEEN FIFTY-NINE was an ominous year of cheap movies, personal appearances and criticism for Jayne. She found herself wondering if people liked her for her "figure" or "as a person."

Her first public appearance was at Carnival in Rio de Janeiro. She was appearing at the elegant Copacabana Hotel. Jayne was undulating about in the ballroom next to the pool when a sizable group of Brazilian men started to remove her dress. "The boys just got a little excited. I really think Brazilians are wonderful, the salt of the earth. I had little red roses on the bosom of my dress. They started picking them. When the flowers were gone they went after the dress. I thought I'd be completely stripped. I was frightened for a few minutes."

Mickey threw his coat around Jayne's shoulders and dragged her away from the crowd. He said, "I was frightened for Jayne for a few minutes. I had a hell of a time getting her out of the dance after I threw the coat over her."

Undaunted, Jayne was on a tabletop with a hula hoop the next day. She spent fifteen minutes working out with the hoop while the crowd yelled "Take it off," referring to her white halter and green shorts. Mickey stood close by to prevent a reoccurrence of the rose-picking incident.

A few days later Jayne refused to visit a nudist colony after her guide, snake dancer Luz del Fuego, explained that she'd have to strip. "It's too bad I'm not Marilyn Monroe," she said. "She's a naturalist. But I would not feel right. I'm sorry." Jayne was undeniably tasteless, but that wasn't the kind of remark she usually made. In a clumsy way she was trying to draw attention away from the bad press and the bad conscience she was getting from the dress-ripping scene. It was one thing, she concluded, to be stripped unwillingly and quite another to volunteer.

She didn't know that she had completed the reputable part of her movie career. But she did know that getting mobbed in Rio was exciting, erotic and momentarily soothing. She relied on this wild, hot, sweaty crowd approval to console her Hollywood disappointments. As an insecure high school girl she had used sex for substitute popularity, and now she was using it for a substitute profession.

Like many women, Jayne was a victim of male sexual fantasies. Men found her exhibitionism desirable. The ef-

○ ○ ○ ○ ○ ○ ○ ○ ○ ○ ○ ○ ○ ○ ○ ○ ○ ○ ○ ○ ○ ○ ○ ○ ○ ○ ○ ○ ○ ○ ○ ○ ○ ○ ○ ○ ○ ○ ○ ○ ○ ○

fect she had on men intoxicated her. Liz Renay, in her autobiography, recalls Jayne and Mickey "balling" at one of her parties. The thrill for Jayne was in watching and being watched.

This behavior frightened her, too. Once she started to work on a crowd she went on and on until things looked dangerous. Mickey was always there, ready to carry her off, but she didn't always want him to. She became dazed by the eroticism of the yelling, tugging, violent crowd. The fear and the denials of complicity came later.

Jayne's favorite word about herself was "crescendo." It describes her particular state of being, one so volatile that neither she, nor Mickey, nor anyone else could contain her sexuality or protect her from some ultimate sexual violence.

Jayne came in for a good deal of criticism, some from none other than Billy Graham. "This country," he said, "knows more about Jayne's statistics than the Second Commandment." Jayne could have chosen to be flattered to be compared indirectly to a graven image, but instead she took up the cudgels.

"I live up to the Ten Commandments one hundred percent. I can't help it if I'm on their minds. It's a free country and a free world and I'm flattered that the youth of the world is thinking about me.

"As far as physical attributes and sex are concerned, one can't help it if one is given by nature and God a certain physical stature and being. And I don't want to change mine.

"I devote a lot of my time to boys' clubs and youth charity and I'm sure that when I attend these clubs I'm looked up to not because of my figure but because of their liking for me as a person.

"I get more fan mail from the seven to twelve age group than I do from the army and navy. That proves I have more to offer than my figure. I feel there is an overemphasis on sex."

Jayne was increasingly on the defensive, protecting herself from all angles of attack, even resorting to the tactics of an eight-year-old ("It's a free country"). Her sexual personality caused her isolation and shame. She couldn't really believe, despite her protestations, that her fame had much to do with her "as a person."

A different woman might have let Mickey come between her and the eroticism she inspired. But Jayne would never stand behind him, rarely relied on him to take care of her or think for her or do for her. She used him to get some things done, but she never needed him to flesh out her identity. Quite the reverse, she gave him parts of her own.

The loneliness didn't come from her power but from the sexual identity she had adopted. Even as it scared her, she had to be wanted. She was at her most vibrant at those times when men wanted things sexual from her. Consequently she developed a highly specialized attitude about men. She counted on them to provide her with a high level of energy and electricity. But she knew men only in relation to her sexuality. She had never developed any tools for finding out much about people, so when she'd exhausted the sex, she'd exhausted the relationship.

By 1959 Jayne probably meant it when she said there was an overemphasis on sex. This overemphasis, which she had made a bargain with, had left her surrounded by people who didn't know her, people who wanted her without knowing who she was. Jayne was sitting by the pool one day with her mother. She was hugging and kissing a Chihuahua with great ardor. "I just love him, Mama," she said. "He's the only one who doesn't want anything from me."

Nineteen fifty-nine was the year Jayne fired her press

○ ○ ○ ○ ○ ○ ○ ○ ○ ○ ○ ○ ○ ○ ○ ○ ○ ○ ○ ○ ○ ○ ○ ○ ○ ○ ○ ○ ○ ○ ○ ○ ○ ○ ○ ○ ○ ○ ○ ○ ○ ○ ○

agent, Jim Byron, and left her agent, Bill Shiffrin. Byron tells his story. "Jayne came to me for instruction. Five years later she said, 'I'm not going to rehire you. We're going to form a corporation.' "

Byron said, "I don't want that. I'm tired of building. It's time for you to go out on your own." He says now, "I was the only guy who ever told her where it was at. Mickey did, too, but he was her husband. I was always the same with her from the beginning to the end. I felt relief, wasn't that upset about it. In retrospect I was upset that I didn't persist and try and guide her because she needed it. Mickey would call up from time to time for Jayne to get me back. I never spoke to her after the end. She needed me. She had fired me and wanted me to start up with her all over again as a corporation with a percentage of her income."

With hindsight, Byron sees their rupture as the beginning of the end for Jayne. "It was her first rejection," he says. It's not at all clear who was doing the rejecting, but it is clear the Jayne had already begun her slide and Byron couldn't have slowed it. In the early years people had criticized Byron's tactics as being undignified, flashy and in poor taste. His tactics, however, were Jayne's tactics, and when she let him go, she retained the strategy without retaining the man who still had some control over it. She wanted to save money.

When Jayne's contract expired at Fox she and Shiffrin parted company. "She was out of my control," he said. "I kissed her off then. She wore me out. She killed all the fire in me. I think she was a better actress than Novak or Monroe. She had a heart. She had emotions. She should have stressed her acting and not her personality. She had talent but after all her tomfoolery no one would buy her."

One of Shiffrin's last experiences with her involved a

bunch of nude photographs. He was violently opposed to their distribution. Mickey said, "Bill, everything you've told her, I absolutely agree with. We've had a terrible argument about these — it may end up in a divorce. You're the only one around this woman who gives a shit. We're the only two honest men and in the end we're going to get killed." Jayne, of course, disregarded their advice, while they were congratulating themselves.

That was the end of the triumvirate which had put Jayne, as Greg Bautzer says, in the curious position of being a "road company Marilyn Monroe." Shiffrin, Byron and Jayne had had an uneven five years, but there had been much that had been fun along the way. Bill remembers calling Byron one day when Jayne was lying on his desk. He told Jim, "I don't know how to say this, but Jayne and I are in love and we're going to get married." "It drove Byron crazy," says Bill laughing. Once Shiffrin got hold of a helicopter, attached a thirteen-foot banner advertising himself and flew over the Fox lot. Jayne complained to him. "You wasted that gag. I could have used it." A few days later, Byron got her a deal opening an industrial development in East Los Angeles. She would earn $4500 for making a personal appearance, but she was in the middle of shooting a film. So Byron got a helicopter, picked Jayne up at the set and returned her forty-five minutes later.

Mickey became Jayne's closest adviser by default. Their professional relationship could never be as easy as Jayne's with Byron. Mickey was genuinely interested in Jayne's career, but he was also interested in his own. He had less talent than Jayne and didn't have her showmanship. Jayne didn't feel that inequity very strongly, but she did object when Mickey advised her on questions of taste and publicity. As second banana, Mickey was dedicated to Jayne's success. Critics would say that he was dedicated to keeping the gravy train moving along its tracks, but Mickey also wanted to keep peace at home. He knew that success made Jayne, and therefore him, happy.

There are those who think Mickey's advice was all bad. Harry Peers says, "He told her to leave Fox and make independent movies about which he knew nothing." But Shiffrin gave her the same advice. Finally, Jayne had to leave because Fox didn't renew her option.

Harry also feels that Mickey was responsible for keeping Jayne from becoming a comedienne and forcing her to remain a sexpot. It should be clear, however, that no one person forced Jayne to do anything of the kind. Mickey liked the sex image, understood it and thought it was good box office. Jayne as a comic mystified him. Partly it was the language barrier. He didn't understand her jokes. (For example, a reporter asked her about her heavy work schedule, wanting to know if she ever took any holidays. "Only on broccoli," she said.) Mickey would smile and shake his head after an explanation. Another more serious problem was that Mickey had virtually no sense of humor.

In the fall of 1959, Jayne made a couple of shabby British films in her first independent ventures. She played "Midnight Franklin," a Soho nightclub dancer, more accurately a stripper, in *Too Hot To Handle* directed by Terence Young. Midnight was in love with Johnny Solo, doomed owner of The Pink Flamingo club. The censors refused to release the movie in this country under its American title, *Playgirl After Dark*. Jayne suggested that someone get a spray gun and cover her offending areas. But the process cost more than the budget of the film.

Jayne starred in *The Challenge* as a brainy gangster lady who masterminds a robbery with Anthony Quayle. She did some topless work in the movie of which she said, "They had to talk to me for three hours to persuade me to

○ ○ ○ ○ ○ ○ ○ ○ ○ ○ ○ ○ ○ ○ ○ ○ ○ ○ ○ ○ ○ ○ ○ ○ ○ ○ ○ ○ ○ ○ ○ ○ ○ ○ ○ ○ ○ ○

do a bedroom sequence without wearing a bra for *The Challenge.*"

Jayne tolerated no opposition from Mickey and he always gave in. He was afraid of losing her, and his fear was real. She craved unanimous, anonymous approval more than she craved him. He was a "square" as Jayne pointed out, but he was usually willing to go along with her. He could generally be found on her publicity junkets. She dazzled him. For her part, she never shared her wild schemes or the spotlight with anyone else.

She and Byron teased him. In Corpus Christi, Jayne was to help the city with its annual Buccaneer Day celebration. Byron says he turned it into Jayne Mansfield Week. When they were traveling around with a motorcycle escort, Jayne turned to Byron and announced that she had to go to the bathroom. Byron told Mickey to pull up to a gas station. Jayne said, "Wait. Let's think about this. When I do it, that man can put up a sign over the ladies' room saying 'Jayne Mansfield peed here.' "

Byron said, "I'll negotiate it."

Jayne said, "Let's bottle it and sell it."

Mickey was bewildered, as he was supposed to be. He was also beginning to disapprove. But he was too slow to catch Jayne. She was always a step ahead of him. And he needed her attention so badly that he put up with the aggravation for the sake of some kind words.

He suffered everything slowly and quietly. Mickey, Jayne and Byron were driving back from a restaurant in Los Angeles to the palace. Mickey had his hand in the open window vent. Byron, by mistake, pushed a button and closed the window. In a minute Mickey said softly, in a strained voice, "Jim, please, my hand."

Mickey the plodder had married a woman faster and smarter than he. Jayne began to tire of his small ideas and small plans. He was eternally fixing the house. He was good at building things and should have been allowed to putter in peace, but Jayne couldn't stand it. Whenever anyone came to the palace, Mickey was carting some boulder around, working on the terracing, the swimming pool or the garden. Jayne's mother likes to minimize Mickey's construction talents. "He never finished anything. He left all the light sockets in the Beverly Hills house unfinished so I had to warn the children away from them."

He did finish the swimming pool. He installed a heart-shaped fireplace of pink Norwegian marble in the living room. He built a white marble fountain which spurted champagne. Jayne gave progress reports. "Mickey tore out all the tile in all thirteen bathrooms. They were just too dreary. Pretty soon the bathrooms will be finished. Then we'll put pink fur on the floor."

He consulted with Jayne about the bedroom. "There will be a heart-shaped red canopy over the bed. On the wall above the bedstead will be cupids and arrows in marble. And all around the bottom of the bed will be pink fluorescent lighting." Mickey saw to all of this.

At the same time that Jayne needed Mickey for his admiration and his plumbing skills, she found him a little ridiculous. She had stunned this great bulk into domestic submission. He was disabled from doing anything but trotting around after her, planting her heart-shaped gardens and looking after her ocelots. Their roles became more and more reversed. Jayne was out earning money, coming home from work tired and Mickey was full of conversation about fixing the door jambs, mowing the grass and the help problem.

Vera Peers thinks Jayne and Mickey weren't "companionable." Mickey was always, "pushing her, idolizing

her. Once he said, 'I'm going to erect a huge marble statue
of you here in the entryway,' and Jayne said, 'Oh, Mickey,
come on.' " Jayne was Mickey's graven image, but his
worship separated them.

Mickey and Jayne were on the road more often than not.
In Blackpool, England, Jayne and Mickey presided at an
evening festival in honor of switching on the sea-front illu-
minations. About twenty thousand people cheered as
Mickey held his eight-month-old son up on his shoulders.
Inspector Frank Seviere of the National Society for the Pre-
vention of Cruelty to Children complained officially. "No
child of that age should take part in publicity stunts, especially at that time of night." It had been a little before 9:00
P.M. Jayne defended herself diplomatically. "Blackpool is
a wonderful family town and I thought everyone would
love to see my baby."

Mickey added, "The boy has been well rested up for the
show. I don't think he was tired."

The mayor of Blackpool sided with the Hargitays. "The
love of Miss Mansfield and her husband for the children
was apparent to all. They are a delightful and devoted
family."

The personal appearance was Jayne's medium. She met
Jet Fore, that year, a man who specialized in personal appearances. Fore is an enormous, voluble, generous man
who does publicity for Twentieth-Century Fox. In 1959 he
managed everything from restaurants to festivals. He
needed a queen for the Palm Springs Desert Rodeo that
year and Jayne agreed to do the honors. In her usual free-
loading way she brought a maid, Mickey and the children
along. Jet drove everybody to Palm Springs and got
stopped on the way for speeding. The cop noticed Jayne,
said he was a fan of hers and asked if he could have an autograph "for his son." Jayne wrote out the autograph, and,

to Jet's utter disgust, the policeman wrote out a ticket. Jet yelled, "Give me that autograph back," as the cop drove off, but Jayne insisted that he be allowed to keep it.

At the rodeo Jayne suffered one of her clothing mishaps. She had squeezed into a pair of skin-tight leather britches so constricting that when she mounted a horse they gave way. She had to wait in a broom closet while Jet had them mended.

Jet liked Jayne, and when, a short time later, he was handling a restaurant in Anaheim, he invited Jayne to make a personal appearance. He offered $1000 for the evening, but Jayne came instead with nine friends who were fed and wined liberally.

Jet was doing PR for a White Front store not long afterward and offered Jayne $1000 in merchandise for an appearance. Jayne showed up, grabbed a shopping cart and started piling things into it. She found toys for Mickey, Jr., underwear for Mickey, Sr., games and clothes for Jayne Marie and jewelry for herself. She filled one cart, asked Jet to push it and filled two more. When she finally pushed her overloaded carts to the cash register, the check-out lady looked dismayed and said, "Miss Mansfield, that's four thousand dollars worth of merchandise." Jayne sailed on through, leaving Jet behind. The clerk asked Jet to stop Jayne. He shrugged and suggested that she stop her herself. In the end no one did. Jayne considered that she was doing White Front a service by denuding its shelves. The White Fronts grumbled but they asked her back.

A reporter asked Jayne why she made so many appearances at supermarkets. "Oh, you're kidding, aren't you? I do it for the money. I get five thousand dollars in cash and five thousand dollars in merchandise."

Jayne was invited to Mexico City where she rode an elephant in a parade. Later, a crowd of twenty thousand

o o o o o o o o o o o o o o o o o o o o o o o o o o o o o o o o o o o o o o

gathered waiting to see Jayne. Mickey, who was skittish, said, "We'll go out the back way." "No," said Jayne. "Those are my fans. It's fine. We'll go right out. They won't hurt us." The Mexicans cleared a path for Jayne but Mickey's clothes got torn.

Jayne was at her best with her fans. Their adoration flowed through her emotional circuits, charging her up. She collaborated with them in an undeniable proof that Hollywood still existed. She provided them with a rich display of fantasies come true. And their devotion assured her that her life was something wonderful. In 1959 the Hollywood fever still hadn't broken and Jayne was one of the few stars still actively trying to infect people with the disease. Not one of her contemporaries or successors so desperately wanted to sustain the image of the old, glamorous Hollywood or would put up with as little privacy to do so.

Jayne's real fans, not the tomato throwers or the rose pickers, were a serious lot, studious collectors and scrapbook keepers. They belonged to her fan club and got monthly bulletins of bogus facts about Jayne's activities and opinions. They read that she and Mickey attended a charity barbecue, that she loved Tchaikovsky, that she ate cottage cheese. They paid twenty-five cents for autographed pictures.

Males had a primary relation with Jayne. She played to them and to their sexual desires. But her true fans were her students, the girls who saw her effect on men. Unlike the males who wanted Jayne the way a groupie wants a rock singer, the girls flattered her by imitation. Adolescent females read her opinions, considered her clothes and surveyed her body. Even sophisticated girls bleached their hair and tried to walk and talk, as Lloyd Price had it, with personality. They experimented with hip wiggling and whispery voices. Jayne was a lesson that achievement depended on a forty-inch bust. From her measurements followed stardom, heart-shaped swimming pools, ermine and admirers. With feelings of envy and despair, girls locked their doors, faced their mirrors and flung their arms back and forth chanting rhythmically,

> "I must
> I must
> I must
> increase
> my bust."

# *1960*

♥ ♥ ♥

IT WAS in 1960 that the country started to cool off. Cool from jazz, the Kennedys, the breeze of irreverence from the northeast. The Beatles were warming up off-stage, ready to come on after Danny and the Juniors. Male styles changed almost overnight. "He's really cool," the girls said. Not about a football player or a motorcycle boy, but about a brain, a folk singer, a political honcho, a preppie or a protohippie. Cool girls wore black tights, black turtlenecks and green jumpers. They carried book bags. The nurds, slide-rule carriers, twinks and grinds were about to inherit the earth. Understatement and phony cynicism were cooler than enthusiasm and frivolity.

From the advanced suburban high schools of New York and California came the beginnings of the sixties. The shock troops of western flower children met the eastern radical paratroopers somewhere over the midwest and exchanged prisoners. The dual invasions reached their opposite coasts and the generation of the sixties came of age, peopled by the political kids, the flower children, the druggies.

o o o o o o o o o o o o o o o o o o o o o o o o o o o o o o o o o o o o

Odd alliances grew up between the believers in change and the fatalists, the militants and the dropped-out each despised and protected each other. Two opposite strains, each based in cool, the one hip, the other activist. They shared a belief in moral innocence, in the innocence of the body and its pleasures, the righteousness of commitment, personal or political. Artifice had no place in the evolution of the decade. For the radicals, dishonesty had given us the war in Indochina, racism and poverty. For the love children, hypocrisy had given us bad marriages, alcoholism, divorce and confused offspring. Love had to go public and sex followed. "Let's fuck" replaced courting rituals, sexual preambles and come-ons.

Jayne was not cool. Funky maybe, and later camp, but never cool. There was no room for her in the major movements of the time. As much as anyone, she represented the moral and sexual dishonesty of the fifties. She stood for titillation rather than honest sexual expression. She was completely artificial, bleach, make-up, tight clothes, fake voice. "I don't think there's a thing I welcome like my Frederick's catalogue," she said. "I don't know what we'd do without it." Jayne's sex-child routine held nothing attractive for the serious and rebellious adolescents of the sixties. So, in her late twenties, Jayne was being relegated to the dirty old man market. She had been judged along with her decade, a period which was reviled almost before it was finished. The major crime of style became blowing your cool, but Jayne wasn't even important enough to deride, never having had any cool of her own to blow.

Jayne and Mickey participated in Bob Hope's Christmas tour, entertaining the boys in Alaska. They were hardly home when Jayne, pregnant again, and the family took off for Rome where she and Mickey shot a mythological epic called *The Loves of Hercules*. Not surprisingly, Mickey played Hercules, well oiled and wearing what seemed to be a very short skating skirt adorned with leather suspenders. Unlike any other male in the movie, Mickey is tanned and greased and so muscle-bound that he can't walk with his arms at his sides but looks like some kind of great, jerky mechanical bear.

The plot, very sketchily, has Mickey's first wife murdered. He sets out to seek revenge, meets a black-haired tribal queen and falls in love in nine minutes. The black-haired queen is played by Jayne, wearing a black wig and a padded bra. It was some kind of gravitational miracle that she didn't fall over with all that frontage on her. At any rate, she and Hercules have to overcome a lot of obstacles to their love, including the murderous impulses of the red-haired Amazon queen who captures Hercules. Jayne plays the Amazon queen in a different wig but the same bra. The movie is dubbed in a variety of accents so that Mickey delivers Shakespearean English, Jayne West Coast American and the others sounds indigenous to locales between Los Angeles and London.

The most outstanding feature of the movie aside from Jayne's bodice is the rampant sadomasochistic element. In an early scene, Jayne, black-wigged, is tied spread-eagled to two trees. Mickey must heave primitive hatchets at her bindings to release her or she will die at his hand. She does a lot of moaning and writhing. In the Amazon sequence, all the women are done up in boots and hardware and get off on torturing men. The Amazon queen's athletic seduction technique leaves Hercules a jelly. He is only manly with the restrained black-haired queen who faints in most of her scenes. Jayne's dual roles were an object lesson in male fantasy. She got to play the demanding, emasculating woman men fear and the demure, passive woman they want.

When the Hargitays returned from Italy, Mickey finished the heart-shaped pool. He had built two heart-shaped islands in its middle and had inscribed "I love you, Jaynie" across the concrete bottom. He said, "It's a monument to our love." Jayne went on, "It's a gift from Mickey because he loves me." He said, "It's been a labor of love and that's priceless."

Meanwhile, Jayne was traveling. The March of Dimes called her to say that they were doing a telethon in Florida and would she help. "Oh," said Jayne, "the March of Dimes is my favorite charity. I can make it to Tampa. My fee is five thousand dollars."

The March of Dimes explained that it did not pay its name guests. Jayne said she'd love to go but couldn't without her fee. The March hung up, but called back and gave in. Jayne then informed it that she couldn't go without her hair stylist, Marc Britton. The March of Dimes heaved a sigh and paid Britton's expenses. Jayne was fifteen hours late getting to Tampa, but she tripled their intake once she was there. She offered a kiss to every man in the audience who would pledge a hundred dollars. When it came to charity sex was no object. The March of Dimes could legalize incipient prostitution for polio. For a change, Jayne couldn't be blamed for doing what she was doing.

Jayne was again in the throes of trying to change her image. Greg Bautzer advised her to get a new look. Her publicity was falling off and her film offers were low quality. Bautzer sent her to Rogers and Cowan, a public relations firm, which agreed to redo Jayne. She was to cover up the cleavage, study acting and elocution and wait patiently for a good part. She told her new counselors that she "wanted to be taken seriously." They planned to send her to the Actors Studio. They changed her make-up. But she couldn't go through with it. "She couldn't stop the nonsense of flying to Montgomery, Alabama, to do a telethon for five hundred dollars," as one agent put it.

o o o o o o o o o o o o o o o o o o o o o o o o o o o o o o o o o o o o o

She flew to Atlanta to appear in a department store. She had a ring of marines around her to keep the crowd back, but the people broke through, pushed Jayne and the marines into a corner and forced them up a flight of stairs. Jayne couldn't get out and remained locked in a room for two hours till the crowd dispersed. She was afraid she'd get hurt. She made trips all across Canada and the south. When she was in Jacksonville, she would say, "Call up the man from Delta. He'll take care of us." She knew publicity people everywhere and always kept their names and phone numbers with her.

Jayne traveled until she was too pregnant. She gave birth to Zoltan Anthony Hargitay, a month prematurely, on August 1, 1960, in St. John's Hospital. That night Vera Peers couldn't sleep. At 10:00 P.M. she heard a voice saying, "Jaynie will call in ten minutes." Vera went into the living room and Jayne called to announce Zoltan's arrival.

The next day at the hospital Jayne told reporters, "I'm just flying. I can't find a cloud to land on." Mickey said, "It's been a long, long wait. We both prayed and prayed." Jayne explained about the name. "Mickey's Hungarian, you know. So we picked a strong masculine Hungarian name, Zoltan, and added the Anthony for sort of balance. Isn't it thrilling?"

It was thrilling for about a month. Babies drew Jayne and Mickey together, but their temperaments and expectations drew them apart. They were fighting. "Non parlo," said Jayne, coming back from Rome after one of their disputes. "You marry him for two years and tell me what went wrong with the marriage," she told one reporter with unusual bluntness. Rome always had a bad influence on Jayne's relations with Mickey, but coming home didn't improve things much. Just as they were about to be named "The Family of the Year" by the Mildred Strauss Child Care Chapter, their marriage started falling apart seriously.

o o o o o o o o o o o o o o o o o o o o o o o o o o o o o o o o o o o

Jayne was cheating on Mickey and drinking too much. One night, for example, she called a friend at 2:00 A.M. She had been fighting with Mickey and drinking. She asked if she could come to her friend's apartment. Mickey got on the phone saying, "You can't let her go. She's been drinking."

No one could stop her and Jayne tore out of the house and arrived at her friend's apartment a half an hour later. She was sitting in her parked Cadillac talking to a policeman. He wanted to give her a ticket but relented when Jayne and her friend assured him that she wasn't going any farther that night. Jayne parked the car and came upstairs. She called a man she knew and he came over. The two of them sat up drinking, talking and laughing all night. Jayne's friend got no sleep and stormed out of the house the next morning. She wouldn't take Jayne's calls all day. That evening, when she got home, Jayne and Mickey showed up to apologize, acting as if nothing unusual had happened.

Jayne drank to alleviate her anxieties about her career and to manufacture some of the excitement which Mickey wasn't providing. When they were in public and Jayne was getting the attention she wanted, she was nice to Mickey. Her sense of public self made her treat him well. But when she was alone with him, bored and dissatisfied, she needled him, pestered him and put him down for being stodgy and square.

Mickey didn't understand the interplay between Jayne's feelings and how Jayne saw herself feeling. He was in love with her despite her vagaries and infidelities. She made sure he remained in love with her, giving him just enough to recall the good times. She couldn't relinquish his devotion any more than she could alienate a fan. So, after their big loud fights they would make up, go to a restaurant and

∘ ∘ ∘ ∘ ∘ ∘ ∘ ∘ ∘ ∘ ∘ ∘ ∘ ∘ ∘ ∘ ∘ ∘ ∘ ∘ ∘ ∘ ∘ ∘ ∘ ∘ ∘ ∘ ∘ ∘ ∘ ∘ ∘ ∘ ∘ ∘ ∘ ∘

coo at each other for a couple of hours. For a day or two everything would be fine.

Things were shaky. Musclemen were on the way out. Mickey's career hadn't advanced since 1957. He had, according to his friend Ross Christena, "subjected" his career to his wife's, but there was precious little to subject. She had kept him replete with publicity, but he hadn't developed anything but his body.

He had imported Christena from Indianapolis to help with a daytime TV show he was starring in. It was a health and exercise clinic. "I will do exercises for the first fifteen minutes of the show and then explain diets. We will also have guests tell us what they have accomplished." Mickey wasn't promising enormous physiques. "This is the wrong conception and I think it's foolish. If someone has an ambition to be the world's best-built man, that's a different story. Then go in for exercises much more. I feel that moderate exercises are the best thing you can do for your health. Nobody ever promised me a title and I don't promise anybody one. People haven't been taking care of themselves. In recent years people have been dying for no reason at all."

Mickey also wanted to open a chain of health clubs, but the project never materialized. He was in the barbell business. Ross was his salesman, but, as Ross explained it, the equipment was impossible to sell because it was chromium and therefore much more expensive than iron weights which lifters usually buy. The weights sat in the cellar despite Mickey's efforts to unload them.

If Mickey wasn't reaching the "tippy top of the highest mountain" Jayne wasn't much ahead of him. She shot a forgettable picture in Rome called *It Happened in Athens*, a drama about a Greek actress who falls in love with a Greek track star, winner of the 1896 Olympic marathon. Try as she would Jayne couldn't justify the film's historical accuracy. "This particular actress I play had platinum hair because she has been to Paris and is up on the latest fashions among film actresses." She amended that to read, "Well, what she has done is copy Jean Harlow and Mae West." Caught again, she said, "Oh dear, well I don't know who was around then but let's face it — none of the pictures today follows history closely. It's good to put glamour in a picture." Those who saw the picture would no doubt agree that *It Happened in Athens* benefited from some glamour. Jayne was also considering a biblical spectacular called *Fabiola*, to feature Christians and lions, but the film was never made.

Jayne described another film it's just as well she never made. "In *Solo* I'm to play a woman who's married to a man that's impotent. It's very dramatic and affords a nice change of pace. I studied dramatics at UCLA, SMU and the University of Texas. I enjoy making films far more than working on the stage. By watching the rushes you can see your work and have it criticized and corrected."

In the fall of 1960, federal authorities filed a tax lien for $6911 against income for the year 1957. The claim prevented Jayne from disposing of any real estate she and Mickey had accumulated. Jayne habitually took her supermarket and bowling fees in cash, thereby not declaring a good proportion of her income. From 1960 on she was regularly in trouble with the IRS.

Despite the unexpected bad luck, and despite Mickey's disapproval, the family had a lavish Christmas that year. Vera and Harry came to celebrate and to see Zoltan. Mickey gave Jayne a slightly used pink Cadillac. Jayne gave her mother a mink coat. Vera was joyful until she tried it on. "Jaynie," she wailed, "you promised to buy me a full-length mink." Jayne said, "Mama, I'll get you another coat."

Jayne and Mickey took the family to the Dunes in Las Vegas right after Christmas. Jayne earned $25,000 and Mickey $1000 a week for an act called "House of Love." Jayne, wearing some sequins on her chest, pursued Mickey, who, clad in pyjamas, was sitting in a huge heart-shaped bed looking at a book by Freud. At the close of the show Mickey swung Jayne around. Opening night her shoulder strap was contrived to break. As columnist Colin McKinlay said, ". . . the skill which went into the design of Miss Mansfield's bras probably impressed the audience the most."

Jayne was worried and depressed. As one of her publicists put it, "The older she got the more insecure she became. The sex thing really does you in. It's frightening. It's got built-in pressures that you don't always create yourself. Writers start saying, 'Well, what'll she be in ten years?' Then you start worrying yourself."

Jayne lied about her age and Jaynie Marie's age. She dressed the little girl up to look eight instead of eleven. She was ten years old for several years. Jayne joked about it, saying, "One of these days you're going to have to start being my sister."

At twenty-eight, Jayne knew that she wasn't going to be America's pin-up girl all her life. Jayne's publicist went on, "She made a lot of pictures that weren't successful so she got to thinking she wasn't going to make it on talent. She tried to do it the other way. Agents lost respect for her. They forgot she had talent because of the schlocky things she'd do. People forgot she was good." Jayne gave her publicist some nude pictures which showed her pubic hair. Jayne was very proud of them. Her publicist destroyed the worst of them and their professional relationship came to an end.

Jayne drank more. Marc Britton accompanied her home from a telethon in the midwest. She drank so much cham-

o o o o o o o o o o o o o o o o o o o o o o o o o o o o o o o o o o o o

pagne in the VIP lounge that she couldn't walk to the plane. Britton went out and bought her a wheelchair and a pair of sunglasses. He wheeled Jayne onto the plane explaining to the stewardess that Jayne was suffering from "exhaustion."

# *Breaking Up Is Hard to Do*

## PART I

IN FEBRUARY of 1962 Jayne and Mickey took a vacation in Nassau. Jayne, Mickey and Jack Drury, publicist for the Gill Hotel chain, went water-skiing. At 5:00 P.M., when Jayne had called a press conference to announce a new picture, the three hadn't returned. A search began at dusk. The next day their boat was found overturned off Rose Island. Some time later, Jayne, Mickey and Drury were found on the eastern beach of that island. Jayne was hospitalized for shock, rock cuts, exposure and sand flea and mosquito bites. She and Mickey both needed hairdressers.

The first question, naturally, was, had it been a publicity stunt? With tears in his eyes, Mickey said, "I am very hurt." Then he started to cry. "If she was to have twin babies, someone would say it was just for publicity. I'd like to take anyone who thinks it was a stunt to that rock for a few hours, not to spend the night like we did — and see how cold it was."

Mickey told a sensational story. Jayne fell off her skis. Hargitay tried to pick her up and fell out of the boat. Jayne panicked. The boat capsized when Mickey and Drury tried to pull Jayne on board. Jayne fainted. Mickey pulled her onto the hull of the boat which drifted to an island. Mickey pulled Jayne onto the island. Jayne fainted. They spent the night on their tiny coral reef. Jayne's life flashed through her mind as she was going down. "I thought of everything I'd done in my life. I thought of my children and my mother. I felt sorry for them. I thought I was going to die. It was the sharks," she sobbed. "That was the worst." Mickey explained that Jayne had a mortal fear of sharks.

Mickey went on. "The water kept getting higher and higher. It kept coming up until I thought it was going to take us. Sitting there like that you think you are going to die." And finally, in an outburst at the reporters, he said, "Jaynie doesn't need publicity. It's a miracle this girl is living today." He said later, "Jayne, brave through the crisis, fell apart after we were safe. That's a woman for you."

Local officials cast doubt over the Hargitays' credibility. The man who found the boat picked it up 400 yards from Rose Island and wondered why he wasn't hailed. The Nassau Yacht Club said there had been no sharks in the waters for many years and that the sea had been perfectly calm for several days.

The likelihood is that Jayne, Mickey and Drury planned the stunt, expecting to be located in time for dinner. Much of Mickey's outrage stemmed from the fact that he hadn't planned to spend a whole night getting bitten by mosquitoes and sand fleas. Jayne and Drury both came away with bad sunburns. Like many of Jayne's ideas, this one got away from her. She recognized that the quality of her press was declining. She was getting coverage but no sympathy. Jayne was surprised and a little dismayed at her treatment.

○ ○ ○ ○ ○ ○ ○ ○ ○ ○ ○ ○ ○ ○ ○ ○ ○ ○ ○ ○ ○ ○ ○ ○ ○ ○ ○ ○ ○ ○ ○ ○ ○ ○ ○ ○ ○ ○ ○

When Jayne and Mickey returned from their ordeal, they went on the road to promote Jayne's new movie, *The George Raft Story*, Jayne's new record, *Jayne Mansfield Busts Up Las Vegas*, and Mickey's barbells. In Chicago she went on every conceivable radio and TV show, met with newsmen all over the city and showed up at various charity functions. At each event Jayne plugged her movie, her record and Mickey's business, Hargitay's Exercise Equipment Corporation. Jayne and Mickey had relatively little to say to each other when they weren't on stage. The only time Mickey perked up was when a gas company asked Jayne if she would pose for pictures to be displayed at gas stations (Miss Fill 'er Up). Mickey asked, "Do we get coupons for lots of free gas?" The answer was yes and he relapsed again into his torpor.

Jayne and Mickey had barely returned to the palace when Jayne filed for a divorce. She startled Mickey. He was out clipping a hedge when reporters arrived to find out his reaction to the suit. He didn't know anything about it and went inside with the newsmen to ask Jayne. She acknowledged that it was true and sent Mickey packing while she went to buy $10,000 worth of clothes from designer Richard ("Mr.") Blackwell, author of the Ten Worst Dressed Women list. She came home and locked herself into the guest room. Eighteen hours later Jayne and Mickey were together by the heart-shaped pool explaining their reunion to an assembly of reporters.

Mickey said, "Jayne has forgiven me. I said I was sorry and all is forgiven. I was wrong. I felt only Jayne and myself should go to Rome rather than take the whole family. Jayne felt I was pressing her away from the children. I certainly knew she loved them but not how much until now. This particular issue has been going on for a month or two."

Jayne took over, saying, "When women bear children

their first obligation is to the children, whether they are movie stars or not. I want the children to know and love me — not a governess. I think Mickey might have been slightly jealous of the children. The whole thing boiled down to him saying, 'I won't go if you take the children.' But Mickey has agreed with me now."

Mickey had no choice, although as principal caretaker of the children he had looked forward to a childless vacation. He also didn't want the children's routines interrupted again, but he was threatened with divorce.

Jayne carried on in an orgy of maternal feeling. "People think I'm a 'symbol of sex' because of my pictures but that's not true in real life. I think a woman's first duty is to her children. I don't want mine growing up like weeds. Career or anything else doesn't carry any weight. I'd rather wash dishes for a living if I have to do that.

"We are all leaving together Monday. I wouldn't be physically able to make a picture without my children. I filed the divorce action because of the conflict between my children and my marriage. I very seriously filed and I certainly intended to get a divorce at that time."

She said she would withdraw the divorce action "as soon as I get around to it. I'm glad because I love Mickey. I loved him just as much when I filed the suit but I had to bring this thing to a decision — and what I considered the right decision."

Jayne, Mickey, the children and Jayne's Mr. Blackwell–designed wardrobe arrived in Rome May 8, 1962. The Hargitays hired themselves a villa and Jayne started to work on *Panic Button*, a movie with Eleanor Parker and Maurice Chevalier. The producer was a forty-two-year-old Italian named, incredibly, Enrico Bomba.

Mickey, the convert, revered American get-up and know-how. He disdained Italian workmen and found himself fretting over new shower nozzles in his Roman home.  Jayne was more concerned with Bomba than the plumbing.

Bomba rapidly became Jayne's lover.  He escorted her around Rome, sometimes *à deux,* sometimes accompanied by a dour Mickey.  The twosome-threesome covered Rome's nightspots and parties.  Things had reached a crisis stage by June 7 when, at a party, Jayne twisted enthusiastically all the way down to her lace bra.  "It was no striptease," she said.  "I just happened to be wearing a very loose-fitting dress.  Occasionally it came apart.  I tried to hold my dress together.  It was the best thing to do in that dress."

Mickey stalked onto the dance floor and tried to remove Jayne.  She and Bomba refused to stop twisting, but Mickey prevailed.  He got Jayne off the floor and into a dark corner where they had a long, loud fight.  Some witnesses claim Mickey hit his wife.  The party began to break up around 3:30 A.M. and Jayne ran, throwing herself into Bomba's car.  Mickey came after her and used some more persuasion to get her into his car and home.

The Italian newspapers were having a swell time.  They called Mickey with a $5000 offer to punch Bomba in the nose providing Mickey would notify photographers of the time and place.  Mickey declined.

American papers noted that Mr. Blackwell was disgusted with his client.  "I can't go on designing for an actress who shows off my work by either having the dresses ripped off her or wrestling on the floor with them.  Besides, I can't stand those shoes she wears — cheap plastic wedgies that went out long ago," he bitched.

In July the family returned to Hollywood.  No one was happy.  Reporters asked Mickey about Bomba.  "I've heard about it but it doesn't make sense because this Bomba is a married man and has two children.  And Bomba isn't the only man after Jayne.  If I lose my wife I lose nothing."

o o o o o o o o o o o o o o o o o o o o o o o o o o o o o o o o o o o o o o o o

Jayne filed again for divorce and her secretary, Rusty Ray, told the press that this time she really intended to go through with it. Jayne was studying to be a Catholic. She changed agents, moving to Elizabeth Taylor's firm, Kurt Frings. Bomba had impressed her with the importance of giving up cheesecake although he wasn't personally averse to it. Jayne was talking again about high-necked dresses, dramatic roles and culture.

The Italian press was bombarding Enrico with questions. Mickey had accused him of sabotaging his marriage, of deceiving Jayne about his marital status and of being broke. Bomba said Mickey's accusations were "absurd. Absolute nonsense. Mr. Hargitay knows perfectly well that I have never tried to sabotage his marriage. Many times I have tried to save the marriage by pouring water on the flames when bitter arguments flared between those two. But it was obvious that their marriage was failing anyway — even before they came to Rome."

Jayne visited Enrico a couple of times in August and signed a contract to do a movie with him called *The Italian Lover*. The title, she allowed, was "meaningful." While they were apart they wrote all the time.

Jayne couldn't read Italian, which made her life more complicated than normal. Publicist Stanley Cowan remembers taking her that summer to make a personal appearance at "a meat-packing concern." In return for her presence Jayne was to get $1000 and 250 lbs. of meat. Cowan borrowed a pink Rolls Royce and drove Jayne and her correspondence into the Valley. Jayne was puzzling over a letter from Bomba and finally stopped at an Italian restaurant and had it translated. Then she had to reply. The Rolls began to overheat and started to issue smoke and steam at the top of some canyon while Jayne was worrying about finding a post office to mail her letter.

After the trip to the meat plant Cowan went to the palace

to discuss some publicity ideas with Jayne.  They had just sat down in the living room when the maid appeared to tell Jayne that Mickey was outside and wanted his clothes. Jayne said he knew where he could find them.  Cowan remembers, "After Mickey gets his clothes, he can't resist coming into the living room where we are talking.  He is very upset.  Jayne makes the introductions and Mickey starts talking to me.

"  'I don't understand this girl, she's so mixed up.  In the bottom of the pool it says Jayne loves Mickey and that crest of arms over there, J & M, means Jayne and Mickey.'

"Jayne stands up and yells, 'Shut your fucking mouth. That doesn't mean Jayne and Mickey, it means Jayne Mansfield.  Now get out of here.' "

One night Jayne got back very late from a publicity tour. Jayne Marie and little Mickey came down for breakfast and as they entered they saw water pouring down from the ceiling under Jayne's bedroom.  Jayne Marie raced upstairs.  A friend, thinking about Monroe's suicide the month before, followed her.  Jayne Marie pulled open Jayne's door to find her mother asleep.  The pipes in her bathroom had burst.  Since it was Saturday and Jayne couldn't find a plumber, she called Mickey.  He was in the middle of an interview but dropped everything to attend to his two major concerns, Jayne and plumbing.  As he fixed the pipes Jayne must have wondered how she could get along without him.  At the same time it must have occurred to her that she didn't really have to.

In August, Jayne had flown home to Dallas for a short visit.  She and Vera had a fight the first night.  Some newsmen made remarks on television about Jayne's separation from Mickey.  Vera tactlessly brought up Marilyn Monroe's suicide.  Jayne said, "They probably expect me to do that some day, but they don't know me well enough to know it couldn't happen," and she ran out of the house.

o o o o o o o o o o o o o o o o o o o o o o o o o o o o o o o o o o o o

Jayne wasn't suicidal, but she wasn't happy. All of a sudden she was in a quandary. For ten years she had been chasing a career. Now it was going nowhere and her sexy act wasn't going to last forever. Mickey had been central to her idea of herself as a romantic woman, as a good wife and mother. He was the keystone of her security. She had come to him, profession in hand, confident of her powers to make their life a traveling triumph. Mickey hadn't changed, but Jayne was running out of steam. She needed some outside source of energy to keep the road show going, and Mickey was engaged in pipefitting.

The slowing down of her career, the attention she wasn't getting prompted her to throw her energies into her private life. Each lover was a statement that she was sexy, desirable, provocative and as exciting as ever. Her public and private needs fused. In her way Jayne never stopped loving Mickey, but his love couldn't reach her. No one could ever fill the hollows of her need. Bomba was a fantasy too. If Carlo Ponti had done it for Sophia Loren, why couldn't Bomba do it for Jayne? Her friend and hairdresser, Marc Britton, said, "She wanted a superintelligent wise type. A Svengali. She wanted good advice so she could be made into a great lady and a film star."

The trouble with Bomba was that he was uncommitted. He was married and unlikely to divorce. Bomba didn't make it absolutely clear at the outset what his intentions were. Nor was he exactly forthcoming about the fact that he was married and intended to stay that way. On the other hand, that was attractive too. A friend of Jayne's observes, "Only constant excitement held her attention. Bomba lasted as long as he did because it was exciting. She didn't know if he was a phony as people said, or whether he would get a divorce. He lasted because she couldn't get him. Everything had to be thrilling. She

○ ○ ○ ○ ○ ○ ○ ○ ○ ○ ○ ○ ○ ○ ○ ○ ○ ○ ○ ○ ○ ○ ○ ○ ○ ○ ○ ○ ○ ○ ○ ○ ○ ○ ○ ○ ○

couldn't stand it if everything went smoothly. She often complicated matters. She needed to be constantly juiced — something had to be happening."

In October Jayne went abroad again. Enrico told the press that he was talking to Jayne about four movies, the first to be shot in Ceylon. Early in the month Jayne left Rome for London, alone and crying. Later, however, she and Enrico were back together again and traveled from Beirut through Rome and on to Paris.

Jayne and Mickey had already signed separation papers and a property settlement. Jayne asked Mickey to meet her in front of the Beverly Hills Hotel to discuss a divorce. Mickey said, "When Jayne asked me for the Mexican divorce my first reaction was to consent. Why try to hold a woman who wants to get rid of you? Then I decided that I have more of a responsibility than that to Jayne. I don't believe she knows what she is doing. I love this country. If she wants to get a divorce in California, that's all right. There would be a year's wait.

"I don't want anything but for Jayne to be happy. When we agreed on the property settlement, I signed away everything. But I'm not going to let Jayne rush into anything that might be foolish."

Harry Peers regards Mickey's generosity with skepticism. "And he claims he gave her everything. He had nothing to give." As for Mickey's patriotism, it was short-lived. He, Jayne and Jerome Lipsky, her lawyer, had an evening meeting a few days later at which Mickey agreed to a Mexican divorce. Jayne said, "I'm in love with Enrico and can't help it. At the end of our talk Mickey made a concession. He said if Enrico came over here, he will agree to the Mexican divorce."

Mickey thought it was a pretty safe bet that Bomba wouldn't show up in this country. "They keep saying he

is coming here. I don't believe it. I think he is scared.
But I am much too much of a gentleman to think of hurting
him. My strength is too big for him."

Bomba, when asked about his impending marriage to
Jayne, said ungallantly, "I'm bored with the subject."

Nevertheless, Jayne announced, "Everything is settled."
They were to be married on April 7 in Paris. "I'm devoting all my time to studying the Italian language, Italian literature and art. I don't go out on dates and I'm going to
bed early every night. I have discovered a beautiful new
world. We will live in Paris for a year or two after the
wedding and then settle down in Italy. There are technical
reasons for this."

Jayne was also devoting some time to Brazilian band-
leader Ivan Morice, but when questioned about him she
answered, "I've never heard of such a man."

The complications facing Mickey in arranging his life
around a divorce were overwhelming. He had to arrange
to see the children. "There must be some way to do it
without Jayne being there." And then there was the ocelot
dilemma. Finally he got permission to board his pet at the
palace. "There is more room at Jayne's and the kids like
him too. This way when I go out to visit the children
. . . I can see Tiger as well."

In a final burst of peevish bravado Mickey said, "I've
had it. I've been patient because I held to the hope that
Jayne and I might get back together, but obviously this is
not going to happen. I'm not calling Jayne any more and I
don't want to see her again. I'm *finita la commèdià* as the
Italians say. I don't know whether those are the exact words
because I'm not studying Italian, I'm studying American.
Anyhow, I'm through with Jayne. But I will date now, in
fact after she gets the Mexican divorce, who knows, I may
beat her to the altar."

For her part, Jayne was suddenly getting coy, saying

things like, "I cannot name the man I will marry for legal reasons."

Bomba appeared in New York just before Christmas. Jayne arranged a romantic little dinner at the Four Seasons with just the two of them and columnist Earl Wilson and his wife. Halfway through the meal Jayne turned to Bomba and said, "I'm not going to marry you. I'm going back to Mickey." Bomba was not thoroughly crushed, but dinner was awkward.

Afterward Jayne got on the phone. Mickey said, "Jayne told me that she never realized how much she really loved me until she saw Bomba on American soil. She said I'm the only man for her. She wants to rush back here tomorrow night and make a happy life for the two of us and our children. I have never stopped loving Jayne. We are going to try to start all over again and forget our trouble. I will meet her at the plane. I think it's a wonderful Christmas present for any family to be together."

It was another splashy, romantic scene for Jayne's collection, strong on drama and weak on reality. She said that Bomba was "the most wonderful man in the world with a beautiful soul and a wonderful heart." She also said, "A woman has a right to change her mind and I'm a woman." Exercising her woman's prerogative, Jayne showed up at the Los Angeles International Airport the next day where she greeted Mickey and thirty-five newsmen. As she said, "Amid cameras and reporters we kissed and swore eternal devotion." To clinch the deal Jayne gave Mickey a puppy.

# Promises, Promises!

♥  ♥  ♥

THROUGHOUT THIS tortuous period with Mickey, Jayne was making other kinds of news.   In Rome she had been knocked down, scratched and kicked by a Spanish dancer named Alma de Rio.   The occasion was a film gala where Jayne was awarded a citation calling her the most popular actress in Italy.   Alma ripped Jayne's evening gown and both women were covered with blood.   Alma was in a snit because she thought she deserved the award.

When she got home, Mr. Blackwell took out after her. He put Jayne on his Ten Worst Dressed Women List and created a special category for her, the Worst Undressed Woman of the Year.   Blackwell, in his critical appraisal of his Worst candidates, mentioned Jayne's habit of wearing bracelets outside her long gloves as particularly offensive.

Jayne, in turn, had some words to say about Mae West. "I've always admired her.   I think that for her age she's doing very well.   And she's smart enough to know that a woman is more attractive when surrounded by men.   I don't care what anyone says, she is still great and a great performer.   But she talks so bad.   I don't mean dirty, I mean bad, like bad grammar."

o o o o o o o o o o o o o o o o o o o o o o o o o o o o o o o o o o o o o o

Mickey and Jayne were working together on a picture called *Promises, Promises!*, directed by and starring Tommy Noonan. The movie is a bedroom farce about a writer (Noonan) and his wife (Jayne) who are on a cruise with their friends, a famous actor (Mickey) and his wife (Marie "The Body" McDonald). Tommy and Jayne want to have a baby, and Jayne takes various concoctions cooked up by the ship's doctor. Tommy, who believes he is sterile, also drinks potency potions. There is a bedroom mix-up, a female impersonator who does Tallulah Bankhead immitations and two short sequences of Jayne thrashing about in bed bra-less, having disturbing dreams. It was because of these sequences that the movie was only shown in "art" theaters. Jet Fore, who was publicist for the movie, had erotic posters of Jayne printed up with a lot of words about the first time ever au naturel for a major star. Each sequence lasts about thirty seconds and bears no relation to the rest of the film which is as clean as a troop of Girl Scouts. Mickey has a breathtaking scene when the famous actor is prevailed upon to display his secret weightlifting talent to the other passengers. Everything works out when both Jayne and Marie become pregnant, despite their husbands' convictions that they are sterile.

One would assume, given that Jayne was making a semiskin movie, that her audience was largely macho. It is a little surprising when one discovers that Jayne's most devoted and loyal fans were gay. One young man has cartons and cartons full of Mansfield memorabilia. He has rare out-of-print paperbacks, clips from every periodical she was ever in, the soundtrack from her Las Vegas appearance in 1963, the soundtrack from a film she made in Germany, a record of her reading poetry, and prints of three of her films, including *Promises, Promises!* He became friends with Jayne when he showed her the enormous scrapbook he had on her.

○ ○ ○ ○ ○ ○ ○ ○ ○ ○ ○ ○ ○ ○ ○ ○ ○ ○ ○ ○ ○ ○ ○ ○ ○ ○ ○ ○ ○ ○ ○ ○ ○ ○ ○ ○ ○ ○ ○ ○ ○ ○ ○ ○ ○

Another gay man, an intimate of Jayne's, regrets now that they didn't marry. He is responsible, he says, for teaching her everything she knew about appreciating male behinds. "We were almost married," says her friend. "We should have been."

And then here is a young New York transvestite who has become Jayne. He dresses up in tight pink outfits, minces and lisps and has changed his name to Mansfield.

A male homosexual friend of Jayne's observed that she had the style and taste of a drag queen. And Jayne's support among gay men grew as her act went from girlish to camp. If one component of male homosexuality is dislike, distrust or fear of female sexuality, it is easy to see why Jayne had a large gay following. She allayed the fears by self-parody, and she shared in the dislike by mocking herself, and, by extension, female sexuality. Jayne blurred the distinction between eroticism and absurdity. In *Promises, Promises!* Jayne, wearing wedgies and skin-tight pedal pushers, straddles an opened door and rubs her calf suggestively up and down against it. One expects the door to moan. It was theater of sex at its most laughable. In nightclubs Jayne went around patting bald men's heads and saying things like, "Do you want me to rub your little nosey-wosey?" and "Does he want his mommy?" She was forced to make a fool of herself, but she intended to put everyone else in the same predicament.

Jayne's interest in comedy increased at the same rate that her sexy act became grotesque. She seemed to enjoy distorting and exaggerating erotic fantasies. Only the very insensitive, blind to the humor and the mockery, could respond to Jayne after a while. She made everyone else uncomfortable.

There is a way in which Jayne seems like a direct antecedent of the transsexual and unisexual vogue of the seventies. It was almost as if she parodied women out of a job.

○ ○ ○ ○ ○ ○ ○ ○ ○ ○ ○ ○ ○ ○ ○ ○ ○ ○ ○ ○ ○ ○ ○ ○ ○ ○ ○ ○ ○ ○ ○ ○ ○ ○ ○ ○ ○ ○ ○ ○

She was the most outlandishly voluptuous, puckered-up sex object of her time, and she made it all a joke. It was as if she was saying, "Look, this is as far as this particular stereotype can be taken. So, what next, women?" She was no longer a feminine model. In fact, her most accurate imitator was a man. She had become too much for straight men to take seriously. She mocked their virility at the same time that she played to them. She was the final word on a certain kind of woman. She married the most heroically built man she could find and turned their life into a traveling sideshow, exhibiting the last survivors of an extinct human breed. She dared the imaginative to go beyond her. Fragmentation set in. Some extremists went in for transsexuality. Sexual exhibitionists, like Linda Lovelace, emerged when their market was allowed to surface. And others just went on doing the same old thing without adding anything to the genre. Raquel Welch, winner of the Hollywood Publicists' Jayne Mansfield prize for exposure in 1969, was doing basic Jayne toned down by "good taste" and dark hair. But Jayne really exterminated the dumb blonde by taking its image to its funny, insane and unpalatable conclusion. She willfully destroyed the fantasy she'd exploited.

During the shooting of *Promises, Promises!,* Hugh Hefner decided he wanted a name star to pose nude for a *Playboy* layout. He got in touch with Charles Block of Globe Photos, who, in turn, got in touch with Tommy Noonan. Noonan, who has been described as having been able to talk an Eskimo into buying a refrigerator, was sure he could convince Jayne to pose nude. He took her to the Brown Derby, fed her champagne and persuaded her. She protested but was won over. The whole process was very similar to seduction. Noonan wooed Jayne, she acquiesced after he assured her that it was all right and he'd still think well of her. After agreeing, Jayne's first question was how much, but *Playboy* and Noonan both felt that the outtakes would be excellent publicity for the movie, of which Jayne owned 10 percent. Jayne agreed to pose for free.

For the first layout, Jet Fore cleared everyone off the set except for the photographers, Marc Britton, and a couple of lighting men. Jayne said to Jet, "Oh, you're here. I'm so embarrassed." Jet started to reassure her but Jayne already had her clothes off.

Jayne asked Marc, "Is Suzi all right?"

Marc looked her over carefully and shook his head. "No, she needs combing." He borrowed Jet's comb and went to work on Jayne's bleached pubic hair. He returned the comb to Jet, who was slack-jawed. A drunken friend subsequently stole the comb from Jet, taking it, he said, for the Smithsonian.

Two days later Jayne and Jet stopped off at the Brown Derby to get primed for the last shots. A local astrologer named Chriswell was at the bar and Jayne said, "So you're the famous predictor. Make me a prediction."

Chriswell said, "You're going to fall in love with an American this year."

"Nonsense," she said, "I only fall for Italians and South Americans." Two weeks later Jayne was in love with American Tommy Noonan.

Jayne and Jet went to the palace to Jayne's pink, furry bedroom where the remaining pictures were taken. Jayne stripped and rolled around on her bed so seductively that Hefner was temporarily enjoined to keep his magazine off the stands since Chicago censors thought Jayne looked as if she were masturbating.

Mickey was unhappy about Jayne's behavior. Whenever he walked into her room she covered up, while the presence of eighteen men hadn't provoked any noticeable mod-

esty. And halfway through the session Jayne called a boyfriend and spoke Italian endearments to him. Mickey
stormed in and went around the room asking everybody if
he was speaking Italian on the phone. Everyone denied it,
but Jet, who said, "Arrivederci." Mickey threw them all
out.

Jayne and Mickey hadn't made much of a reconciliation.
Jayne spent her evenings at the Frascati Grill on Sunset
Boulevard, where she listened to pianist Marty Rocklin
play *Fly Me to the Moon* over and over. She drank a lot.
She was a dangerous driver and an out of control lover.
One friend persuaded her to let him drive her home. She
was wearing a long mink coat and had taken off everything
else. When they pulled into the driveway she took off the
coat and dragged it along behind her into the house. She
staggered up to her room and tried to keep her friend
there, but he left after she passed out.

Early in February Jayne told newsmen that the marriage
was over again. "The reconciliation just hasn't worked out
and although Mickey and I get along very well, I plan to get
a divorce as soon as I have time to work out the details.
It's definitely over."

Mickey said, "This was a surprise to me. The way I feel
is this — I have tried to work it out so it would be smooth
with us again. I forgave Jayne everything she did. I tried
my best, but if that's the way she feels, I don't see any
reason to drag it out longer. I am going to see my attorney, Merle Horwitz, today and I plan to file for a divorce as
soon as possible. I don't know the details yet or what will
change.

"The only thing I'm going to ask is that Jayne put my
share of the house in a trust fund for the children. Our
house is worth about a half a million dollars. I don't want
anything for myself. I can stand on my own. I have since

I was a boy, but I feel it is wise to protect our children.
Jayne has been a wonderful mother to them, but I would
like to see their financial future assured."

A day later Jayne called Mickey from the Miami airport
to say that she was upset "when she made those remarks
in New York about marriage."

The next week a Beverly Hills hairdresser and friend of
Jayne's, Lynn Hardy, alleged that Mickey had beaten him
up at 3:00 A.M., February 27. Hardy had given a cocktail
party after which all the guests had gone out to dinner.
Everyone but Jayne went back to Hardy's apartment. She
and Hardy sat for a few minutes in her car saying good
night. According to Hardy, Mickey opened the car door
and began hitting him. Jayne was knocked to the street.

Mickey said, "How can the man make up things like
that?"

Jayne said, "Let's just say this. I had been to dinner
with some very nice people. When this rough stuff started
I thought I had better get out of there. I did. I didn't see
who the other man was. I still don't know. I'm not speaking to either of them at the moment."

About the divorce, Mickey said, "We'll just have to see
what happens. There is also another thing to be considered. We still have another scene to do together for our
picture *Promises, Promises!*"

On the set Jayne was oblivious to Mickey. He followed
her around, carrying her towels when she wasn't wearing
them. But Jayne was engrossed with Noonan. She would
call him at home and he would fabricate conversations
about the movie for his wife's benefit.

After the picture was finished Noonan talked Mickey
into letting Jayne go to Palm Springs with him. Mickey
was baffled but agreed that it would be good promotion for
the picture. Jet went along covering for Jayne and
Tommy. The affair lasted about four weeks.

In April Jayne was in Biloxi, Mississippi, playing, ironically, at the Gus Stevens Supper Club, the place she was working when she was killed four years later. She confided in Louella Parsons. "I've been thinking it over and weighing our problems for more than a year, and I think it's better we go our own ways. Mickey has his TV show and some motion picture commitments and it won't work any hardship on him. I think it's better for the children. When there isn't love and affection between the parents, it's very injurious to the children." Jayne had all three kids with her at the time.

A consideration which helped Jayne make up her mind was a Brazilian named Nelson Sardelli, who was singing with her in Biloxi when he wasn't kissing her ankles. He and Jayne had played together in Buffalo and he had been with her on her southern tour.

Jayne announced to the press that she wanted Mickey's towels out of her bathroom. Mickey complained that he was the "last to learn" of her wishes.

Jerry Schutzbank of Bautzer's office said on April 22, "Jayne Mansfield's signed application for divorce is now in the mail to an attorney in Juarez. We're requesting a hearing for next Monday."

Mickey said, "I previously signed papers agreeing for her to get the decrees in Mexico if that is how she wants it."

Jayne and Sardelli flew from El Paso to Juarez on April 30. Gomez Trevino, Jayne's Mexican lawyer, filed for Jayne on May 1 at the First Civil Court. When the divorce was granted Jayne told Trevino she'd see him in ten years. He said, "Make it three and I'll give you a discount."

Jayne shrugged off questions about her future plans. "It's been all over for Mickey and me for a long time. I just haven't had any peace of mind. But I do now. I feel better about it."

Sardelli told reporters that "we are deeply in love." He hoped for a church wedding, despite the fact that he already had a wife. Jayne, on the other hand, said she wasn't free and "couldn't make any announcement of future plans." She said Sardelli was "a wonderful singer and we expect to make a number of other nightclub appearances together."

Sardelli, en route from Juarez to Dallas, is reported to have said, "Boy, I wish Hargitay were here to help with the baggage."

When Jayne and Nelson arrived at the palace, Mickey had only left an hour before. Sardelli kissed Jayne on the ankle and said, "You are the most beautiful girl in the world."

"Thank you, my treasure. I've met many men in my life," Jayne went on expansively, "and Nelson is one of the most wonderful. He has a beautiful heart and mind and body — and he's got dimples too."

Mickey said, "I'll probably stay with a friend. I've tried to keep up my end of the marriage. I've stuck by Jayne, but, if she wanted a divorce, there was no point in fighting her. I signed over everything to her. I just want her to be happy."

Jayne, equally magnanimous, said, "It's not for me to ask when Mickey will get his things out. He is welcome to leave them there as long as he likes. I laugh and joke now but when I stop I have a numb feeling in my heart."

Sardelli, also anxious to be decent, volunteered, "I did not say I wish Hargitay were here to help with the baggage. It is not in my taste of character. Though I have never met the gentleman I have the deepest respect for him. I just don't find it in my heart to say anything that would increase his present sorrow."

The affair with Sardelli drew to a close. Two days later,

Jayne was making a personal appearance at the Walnut Creek Supermarket in Concord, California. Rusty Ray ordered Sardelli out of Jayne's hotel room where they had been fighting after a press reception. Sardelli punched Ray, gave him a bloody nose and a black eye and left immediately for San Francisco. Jayne was weeping but managed to say that Sardelli was a "nice guy." She also said she and Sardelli were to have gone to Macon, Georgia, the next day where she was to appear in a two-day telethon. She went by herself.

That summer Jayne went to Germany where she made a movie called *Heimweh nach St. Paul,* or *Homesick for St. Paul* with a German rock star named Freddy Quinn, an Elvis Presley imitator. It is a musical in which Jayne sang a couple of songs in German with glockenspiels and accordions in the background. In this country the film was released only in a couple of theaters in Yorktown, the German section of New York City. While Jayne was in Munich she wrote her friends that she was very upset, confused and unsure of herself. One of the things that was on her mind was that she was pregnant.

Jayne decided to get in touch with Mickey, who came over with the kids. Together they all traveled to Budapest to collect Mickey's mama. Jayne announced her pregnancy there, saying that she and Mickey were still legally married in California although divorced in Mexico and that they had planned to have the child all along. Most sources agree that the baby was Sardelli's, but Jayne stuck by her story and she and Mickey did seem reunited. They returned to the United States and installed Mama Hargitay in the palace.

Jayne and Mickey left Mama with the kids and went to Las Vegas where they were rehearsing a show for the Dunes. Jayne was also shooting a movie eventually re-

leased as *Spree*. It's a Las Vegas travelogue with Vic Da-
mone and Juliet Prowse in which Jayne does a strip and
sings "Promise Her Anything."

Jayne elaborated on her Dunes act. "Deep inside every
woman there are certain devices designed to attract a
man — devices to attract a man's eyes to what he should
be attracted to. I've always sensed this — been aware of
it, in my dress and the way I walk. Well, in this strip I do, I
have a perfect chance to attract men's eyes, so I want to be
just right. It's a challenge."

Jayne got a standing ovation after her dress (or undress)
rehearsal strip. "It's wonderful. I've always thought it's
the role of women to spread sex and sunshine in the lives
of men. This was the perfect way to do it.

"I know the experts say a girl can be just as sexy in high-
necked dresses, but that's the hard way. If handled
tastefully, cleavage seldom fails. It's the easiest way to get
eyes focused on the right places."

Then executing one of those unparalleled non sequiturs
Jayne divulged that she was becoming a Catholic: "I'm in
Europe about six months of the year. There I go to Mass
every Sunday and to church every day of the week, even if
it's just kneeling on the steps. Here I always slip out to
church between shows. — I was going to marry Bomba. I
seriously took up Catholicism then."

She said that Catholicism had saved her marriage, "although I did try to divorce Mickey. And it was religion
that brought me to Sardelli. He's a fine person, a religious
person. Once he was going to be a priest. He may become one yet. He said to me, 'If you leave me, I'll enter
the priesthood.' " Sardelli, who lives outside Las Vegas,
has not taken the cloth.

Jayne continued. "It governs my life. It guides my
thinking and acting. It's something nice. I like it. It gives
me peace. With my crazy hours, most churches are closed

when I'm up and around. But if I can just kneel on the steps and hold someone's hand, His hand, things have a way of working out. I'm religious because I *need* it."

Jayne tried to reconcile her religious conviction with her sex image. "A woman should be all things. I'm a mother first, and a good mother. Then I'm an actress. And finally a sex symbol. Each is divorced from the other." The *Playboy* pictures "were distributed without my consent, approval or agreement. They were taken by a staff photographer on the set of a movie. They were supposed to have been screened by the publicity man . . . Those pictures were sneaked to *Playboy*. I knew they were being taken but I was told they were only for foreign consumption. Europeans have a much more adult outlook on nudity than Americans."

Being all things is a familiar woman's problem. A woman has to be the best wife and mother, housekeeper, cook and efficiency expert, particularly if she is to justify working. The fragmentation was so apparent in Jayne's life because her roles were so exaggerated. But the effect on her was as strong as, perhaps stronger than, that on any woman required to be motherly, wifely, sexy, capable, practical, sentimental, provocative, soothing, determined, self-effacing, forceful and so on.

An additionally confusing factor was that Jayne's opinion of herself varied with her audience's. And she couldn't abide the thought that there might be someone, somewhere, who didn't love her. She had to be all things to all people, *Playboy* subscribers and the Women's Christian Temperance Union alike.

If she failed to make someone love her she'd failed as a woman. She said, "It's funny about me and men. Once I start something with a man, I can't just stop and get rid of him. Every man I have been with remains very much in love with me long after I've lost interest. If I want to break it off, if I insist it's over, they hang on.  I hate it.  It's not pleasant."

Jayne didn't select men individually, she chose them all. She didn't want to know them, she wanted to attract them. She and her lovers were the victims of her need.  Jayne couldn't allow people to lose interest in her.  She held on to old boyfriends just as she held on to Mickey.  He never left her because in between the insults and the cheating she fed him enough tenderness and hope so that he believed that there was reason to hang around.

When *Promises, Promises!* came out it was banned in Cleveland.  In defense of herself Jayne said, "If you knew me, you'd find me on the prudish side . . . This picture of mine happens to be quite innocent."  She said she wouldn't allow her children to see it.  "I wouldn't let them drink martinis or smoke cigarettes.  Those things are for adults."  In a more pugnacious mood, she said, "There are two scenes in which I appear nude for a brief moment. The only objections I've heard are that the scenes are not long enough."

Jayne produced a record that year called *Shakespeare, Tchaikovsky and Me* on which she read love poems to an accompaniment of strings.  "I can think of no greater beauty than the reading of a Shakespeare sonnet with a background of Tchaikovsky's romantic and beautifully poetic music.  It is like a great Broadway musical with words and music by the Masters."  She read dozens of poems including, of course, "How Do I Love Thee?," "If This Be Love," "She Walks in Beauty," "Was This the Face," "To the Virgins, to Make Much of Time."  She read with enthusiasm and a lisp.

The year closed on the same note as it had opened. Mickey and Jayne didn't know what was going on between them.  Jayne said, "It's an interesting situation.  My lawyer is questioning the validity of the divorce.  Something

○ ○ ○ ○ ○ ○ ○ ○ ○ ○ ○ ○ ○ ○ ○ ○ ○ ○ ○ ○ ○ ○ ○ ○ ○ ○ ○ ○ ○ ○ ○ ○ ○ ○ ○ ○ ○ ○ ○ ○ ○ ○

about the papers not having been filed correctly. Mickey and I kind of hope they're not valid."

She said their troubles began over the children. "Our personalities are different. I am easygoing, I avoid arguments. I can't stand unpleasantness or discord. Mickey is wonderful, devoted, a good husband, but he is Hungarian! He flares up and boils over. Also, he's very strict with the children. I'm soft with them. Yes, it started with the kids. Although people do say they're the best-behaved kids they've ever seen."

Mickey wanted obedience and Jayne wanted love. Jayne's third husband, Matt Cimber, who is not the most charitable source on the topic of Mickey, says he was sitting around the Hargitay-Mansfield pool one day. Zoltan had made a bowel movement in his pants. Mickey took the dirty pants, turned them upside-down on Zoltan's head and told him to walk around that way for half an hour. "You will never do it again," he told his three-year-old son. Matt claims to have swung at Mickey and, for his trouble, broken his own arm.

Jayne had other complaints about Mickey, however. "Mickey was a perfect physical specimen and I was very physically attracted to him. I'm a girl who likes hairy men, and the only thing I had against Mickey on the physical side of our life was that he didn't have a single hair on his chest.

"But there was a much more serious disadvantage. I'm a girl with an IQ of one hundred and sixty-three and I need someone with whom I have an intellectual attachment.

"For instance, I wanted to study Italian and French literature and Mickey couldn't care less about things like that."

Mickey concluded that a divorce wouldn't hurt the children. Unusually dense, he said, "I don't think divorce upsets young kids. Children are strange. As long as they're fed, dressed and allowed to play, that's all they worry about. Divorce is the worse thing that can happen to a man and his wife. But even worse than that is staying together for the children's sake.

"I feel the worse thing that can happen to kids is to see their parents unhappy. I do my kids a favor — if I can't get along with my wife — to get a divorce.

"One of our troubles is that Jayne and I wanted a large family. Quickly we had Miki, then Zoltan, then too much time went by without another baby. If she'd been pregnant there'd be no divorce. She adores kids — she wants three, four, five, seven, ten babies. And I knew she wanted lots of kids when I married her."

# Matt Cimber

♥ ♥ ♥

JAYNE GAVE BIRTH to a baby girl on January 23, 1964. She was born at St. John's Hospital and weighed 8 lbs. 9 oz. Mickey was very happy. "We are tickled to death that it's a girl. She's the cutest little thing. We have a name for her, but I think I'll let Jayne give it to you when she wakes up." Jayne announced that the baby was Mariska Magdolna, after Mickey's mother. Two days later she was home from the hospital saying, "Mickey and I are looking forward to our next baby. Mariska is such a darling. She has blue eyes and a pug nose like mine. Jaynie Marie and I are playing dolls. We are dressing her and putting booties on her. We are so elated."

Jayne didn't get pregnant fast enough to save the marriage again. Instead she and Mickey went to the Peppermint West to twist, less than a month after Mariska's birth. Mickey said, "She is deeply religious in many ways but is one of the best twisters in the country. She does not consider it undignified or forbidden." After many hours of twisting, Jayne slapped Mickey and headed out of the bar with a man. Mickey ran after them, shoved the man, and Jayne fell to the pavement. Mickey picked her up and took her to a phone booth where she sat crying till he drove up in his convertible and took her away.

Mickey and Jayne denied the story. "I never fight," he said. "I'm a lover at heart. I'm not a fighter." Jayne said, "I didn't slap Mickey. I wouldn't do that. I may have given him an affectionate tap on the face but that's all."

Mickey described the evening. "We all stayed inside a while, then Jayne went to the powder room. In about five or ten minutes, the doorman came by and said Jayne wanted to go home. I went out and someone drew my attention to Jayne and some fellow walking with her about a half a block away. I walked up to them and asked Jayne where she was going. I said to this fellow, 'Thank you very much. I have a car of my own.' That's when she slipped and I helped her up. Since it was raining and a telephone booth was nearby I asked Jayne to sit inside and not get wet anymore while I got the car."

The next day they flew to Spain. Friends quoted Mickey as being angry with Jayne for going out with "another Latin lover type." He hadn't, it turned out, seen anything yet.

When Jayne got home she and the family drove east, where she was doing summer stock. In May, Jayne was starring in *Bus Stop* in Yonkers, New York. Mickey had a secondary part and the director was a stocky young man named Matt Cimber, originally Thomas Vitale Ottaviano. Cimber is an intense and volatile man who electrified Jayne. He stood in sharp contrast to the phlegmatic Mickey. Cimber was twenty-eight and, Jayne raved, "also has the most beautiful physique I've ever seen, aesthetically speaking." Still speaking aesthetically, "He looked like a Greek god's statue." There was more. "He's way beyond a genius. He'd never married even once . . ." Even better than that he claimed an IQ of 165, two points higher than the one Jayne prescribed for herself. She didn't take to Cimber immediately. "I was really turned off when I met him the first day. By the second day he had turned me on."

Cimber says now, sitting in the Polo Lounge of the Beverly Hills Hotel, "It wasn't a great romance, but we made each other laugh." He sips a Coke and looks around the room through his pink glasses. He gives the headwaiter a wad of bills and leaves.

Cimber is a dark, heavy-set man of medium height. He changed his name after he left Brooklyn and went to the University of Syracuse because he was hanging around with Anglo-Saxon types. He drives his chocolate brown Mercedes, with a phone between the seats, to one of his two offices in Los Angeles. Matt is a very successful pornographer. His films include *The Sensuous Woman, He and She, Man and Wife* and *Black African Sexual Power*. His office is a nondescript two-story house decorated absent-mindedly with posters from Matt's movies, including one of Mickey's pornographic efforts called *Delerium*. Cimber occasionally distributes films for Hargitay. "I bought one film," he says laughing, "and practically stole the other." Cimber makes a phone call. He is trying to promote some motorcycles to be used in his film, *The Black Six*, a violent moral tale about six black Vietnam veterans who take up bikes and nihilism. They are provoked into battle by a regiment of racist rednecks. The film features chain beatings and gas tank explosions and stars six black football players. Former Olympic star Rafer Johnson advised Matt on direction. Matt sits behind a big black desk, clear except for two pictures of his little boys and several telephones. When the cycles are secured he goes next door to his movie theater, which is showing *Deep Throat*. He checks with the ticket seller and drives on to Cyrano's, an Italian restaurant on the Strip.

Cimber orders a Coke and starts talking about Mickey.

Matt has a low opinion of Mickey's competence and enjoys outwitting him. "I sold him about fifteen thousand square feet which he and Jayne had paid forty-seven thousand dollars for after I checked with the city to make sure it couldn't be used for anything. A fucking mountain." Matt says Mickey is so stingy that he feeds his children bologna sandwiches. Every time he talks to the third Mrs. Hargitay he asks her about the bologna. Mickey, Matt says, opened a topless bar and couldn't make a go of it. The reason, says Matt, who opened the successful Puss 'n' Boots bar, was that Mickey was too cheap to pay the bartender a good salary. Consequently Mickey got cheated. The moral lesson is that it's worth good money to treat the help right, particularly when the help is handling your good money. Matt continues, saying that Mickey brought him a film script for advice. Mickey had written a story called *The Weird Ones*, which Matt thought was terrible but which he praised to confuse him. Matt holds a grudge for a long time. He holds it against Mickey that Matt has always been billed as the villain in Jayne's life, her great mistake. If only, everyone still says, she had stayed with Mickey who loved her instead of taking up with that low-life opportunist. Matt has never set out to be popular. He prefers power to popularity. He has managed to secure a position where he feels he can humiliate Mickey in small ways. He takes satisfaction in maintaining their strained intimacy.

Matt is a man of habit. He has been going to the same clubs and restaurants for years. And he's been telling the same stories. He made these remarks in 1973. Three years before, he told Carolyn See, author of *Blue Money*, a witty and perceptive book on pornographers, the same incidents.

Matt leaves Cyrano's and drives down the Strip to La Taverna, an Italian nightclub. He sits down and orders a

Coke when a friend of his walks in, a twenty-one-year-old woman in turquoise and feathers. She is, she explains, hoping to find Johnny Carson who has recently broken her heart by marrying. She has spent the afternoon drinking with Matt's wife, Christy, and is a little unsteady. The club's singer, a down-at-the-heels Sinatra type, finishes his set and comes over to sit with Matt. They speak rapidly in Sicilian. The woman is restless and wants to track down Carson. Matt pays for everyone's drinks and drives to a private club in Beverly Hills. The young woman is a member and signs for Matt. She goes immediately to the bar and Matt watches the backgammon players, men in white ducks and madras jackets. In his floral shirt, suede jacket, pink glasses and soft boots, Matt looks like a publicist for a rock group who got invited to a Grosse Pointe party by mistake. He enjoys the warm greetings his friend gets and seems to enjoy equally the coolness toward him. His wife is a society woman and liquor heiress and these are her friends, not his.

Carson doesn't show up and Matt drives his friend home so she won't wrack up her $11,000 Mercedes sports car. At the entrance to her husband's enormous house, Matt pauses while his friend pushes a button on the dashboard and the gates of the driveway open. Matt picks up his own car and drives to a middle-eastern restaurant back on the Strip for a late dinner. Before he orders he negotiates with the owner to buy the restaurant. He likes the location and wants to set up his friend the singer with a good spot. He and the owner exchange information and arrange a meeting. After dinner Matt goes to an Italian bar-restaurant where the singer is drinking. The singer introduces Matt to a Sicilian from Chicago who wears a diamond pinkie ring and looks a little like Liberace. The two greet each other warmly and speak Sicilian for half an hour. At 2:30 A.M. the man from Chicago leaves. Matt

o o o o o o o o o o o o o o o o o o o o o o o o o o o o o o o o o o o o o o o o o

pays for everybody's drinks and drives home to his house in Laurel Canyon.

Cimber's charm lies in his energy and directness. He is not romantic and has no use for tact. Cynicism comes naturally to him. He is crafty and ambitious. He makes a habit, for example, of observing people from a hiding place before meeting them. It took him one day to size up Jayne's weaknesses and potential. One of the things he learned was that Jayne was a strong, dominating woman, tired of her strength. At least for a while she was ready to be ruled. She had controlled Mickey so long that he had become contemptible, and that contempt had infected her view of herself.

Jayne found something cleansing in Matt's arrogance. She was no longer responsible. He would take on the burden of her life. She said, using the same words she'd used about Bomba, "He will be to me what Carlo Ponti is to Sophia Loren. He'll manage and direct me in the more serious things I'll do now in the Fellini–De Sica vein."

Cimber recognized that Jayne wanted someone to take over. He became her manager as fast as he became her lover. "I never made a mistake with her career. I made a lot of other mistakes, but never with her career." Other people have different judgments, but it was that self-confidence which won Jayne.

That summer Jayne and Matt carried on their affair while Mickey trailed around with the kids. According to Matt, he and Jayne got married "because we woke up one morning and thought, why not? The circumstances were comfortable. I was managing her." He told Carolyn See, "She wanted to settle down, I said O.K. . . . For a long time before we got married we weren't even making it. I'd come back from a date, four in the morning we'd meet someplace and compare notes and *laugh*. I'd always be able to say something that would crack her up."

○ ○ ○ ○ ○ ○ ○ ○ ○ ○ ○ ○ ○ ○ ○ ○ ○ ○ ○ ○ ○ ○ ○ ○ ○ ○ ○ ○ ○ ○ ○ ○ ○ ○ ○ ○ ○ ○ ○ ○

Cimber is a careful man and consults lawyers the way most people consult the weather bureau. He knew that marrying Jayne was going to be one complicated maneuver. There was the serious question about the validity of Jayne and Mickey's Juarez divorce.

Mickey's attitude was, "I don't want to fight Jayne if she wants to marry her new manager, God bless her and I hope she is happy all the rest of her life. But that Mexican divorce is not a clear-cut deal. I'm trying to buy some property to subdivide. They tell me I'll have to have my wife's signature. I tried to tell them I have no wife. They say they are sorry but they are not sure of the legality of the Juarez divorce.

"The whole thing is frustrating. After Jayne got her freedom in Mexico, she came to me and said she didn't believe it was legal. We went back together. We had a baby. I bought property as a married man. Then Jayne met Cimber. A few weeks later she told me the divorce was legal. Fine! Any way she wants it. But I have to have some definite ruling so, at least, I can carry on my business."

Jayne's attorney, Richard E. Meyer, testified two months after Jayne's death that Mickey, in August of 1964, had asked Jayne for $25,000, two pieces of real estate in Los Angeles and nine other lots. Jayne and Mickey's lawyers got together and drew up an agreement dated October 26, 1964, giving Mickey $10,000 and several of the properties.

On August 26, 1964, Jayne filed suit in Superior Court for California recognition of her Mexican divorce. She also sought exclusive custody of Miklos, Zoltan and Mariska.

One of the few private acts of Jayne's life was marrying Cimber. After he had made sure the marriage would stand up they flew with only one witness, Matt's lawyer, to Baja California, where they were married on September 24, 1964.

A week later, one of Mickey's lawyers, Jerome Weber,

o o o o o o o o o o o o o o o o o o o o o o o o o o o o o o o o o o o o o o o

said, "I don't think Jayne's Mexican divorce from Mickey was legal. I imagine she had her doubts too because she brought action in Superior Court here to ask that it be upheld. Mickey is contesting this. We're going to look into the matter and we'll decide whether to seek custody of the children."

By the end of the month, Mickey had given up the notion of a custody suit. Jayne, confident of Matt's ability to steer her through the ugly repercussions of her disordered past, settled down to more traditional newlywed pastimes.

Matt gave Jayne a red Ferrari and a town house at 52 East 69th Street in New York. Jayne said, "It won't have anything pink or heart-shaped except me."

Just after the wedding Jayne and Matt flew to Dallas, where Vera and Harry had a reception for them. The pair stood around accepting congratulations after which the conversation turned to race. Cimber recalls with a mixture of bitterness and humor, "If they were talking about niggers in front of my face, I knew they were talking about guineas and wops when my back was turned. So I turned to a lady who was standing next to me and asked her in a very loud voice if she'd heard about Jayne's next movie with the nude scene she does with Sammy Davis, Jr. The party got very quiet and we left after a few minutes."

Cimber is not a great favorite with the Peers. "I hope," Vera says, "I'll never hear that name again." They think he was "no good" and hint at evil secrets which they will carry to their graves. Actually, they know very little about Jayne's life with Cimber. She visited them infrequently, was aware of their disapproval and didn't confide in them. They were not encouraged to visit.

Before moving into their town house in New York, Jayne and Matt went to California to collect the kids and whatever Jayne needed from the palace. Mickey was in and out of the house and Matt remembers that Maria (Jayne made

Mariska's name Italian when she married Cimber) was very sick, with a high temperature. "Jayne and Mickey," says Matt, "are having a huge fight. Maria is upstairs with a fever of one hundred and six degrees and they are fighting about who is going to call the doctor." Matt is wearing a cast on his right arm, having broken it when he punched Mickey earlier that day for disciplining Zoltan. "With the cast I dial a doctor. Mickey yells, 'Put that phone down.' He comes charging across the room. It's a huge room. I'm very slow with the cast but I grab a piece of statuary and clobber Mickey on the head with it. He goes right out."

There was *Sturm und Drang* all over the place when Matt and Mickey got together. The next time they met was at a brawl on Fifth Avenue and 72nd Street in New York. Mickey had flown in from Rome where he was making one of his body movies. He stopped off in New York to see his sons. Jayne agreed to meet Mickey but said she didn't want any photographers. "I didn't want to help publicize Mickey's new career as a European film player," she commented. Matt went on, "Mickey shows up with hundreds of photographers and I haul off and slug him."

The newspaper account has Mickey grabbing Zoltan, Matt stepping in, punches being thrown but not landing. Matt said, "I'm not scared of that muscleman. I come from Brooklyn. I can knock his capped teeth off. He belongs in a tree."

Mickey: "Zoltan jumped into my arms and Cimber swung at me. I told him, 'If I swing at you, you'll be sorry.' A friend of mine told me to forget it and I walked away. Jayne is a wonderful girl but he's impossible. She's made of gold. Her husband is equal to zero. I love her as my children's mother."

Jayne: "He's not so tough. My male secretary beat him up once. I have been receiving love letters from this fellow even though I'm happily married. He's made many phone calls to me. Of course I've shown these letters to my husband. I paid ten thousand dollars as a settlement for this big muscleman. I also paid up all his debts. I've never been so happy. I always dreamed about falling in love. I didn't think it existed, but I was wrong. I never knew it was possible to be so happy."

Mickey: "There must be some easier way to see my children than to have a fight. I have called my L.A. attorney, Merle Horwitz, to take the necessary steps. I didn't know any photographers were going to be there. I did not see any while I was waiting."

Some trio: Matt's threatening Brooklyn bass, Mickey's grieved Hungarian tenor and Jayne's breathless high school soprano. Jayne had picked up Matt's habit of sneering at Mickey's muscles, which she had been so wide-eyed about not so long ago. Matt, in his zeal to make Mickey look foolish, came off like a moron. Mickey needed no help to sound ridiculous. He was hurt by Jayne's remarriage. He was pugnacious too and harassed the Cimbers. He allegedly kidnapped Maria for three days in August of 1964 to force Jayne home. In all of his behavior there was a need to get Jayne's attention. "Notice me, notice me," he seemed to be saying, like a child waving his hand in the back row who has got the answer and wants to be called on.

Jayne, for her part, was in the throes of her I've-never-been-in-love-before routine. But the words stuck in her throat. She was in the awkward position that the Soviet Union found itself in when it had to de-Stalinize. Jayne had to renounce Mickey as throughly as she had once exalted him and ring in a new dictator.

In keeping with her flourishing romance she became pregnant in January. Cimber said to Louella Parsons, "Everything good is happening to us."

# The Playboy Philosophy

♥ ♥ ♥

AT THE TIME that Jayne met Matt, she was involved in a controversy over *Playboy*'s use of the *Promises, Promises!* pictures. Jayne had a long-standing relationship with *Playboy*. Their association began in February 1955 when Jayne modeled in pyjamas raised so that the bottoms of her breasts showed. Shortly afterward she posed for the *Playboy* calendar covering her breasts with her hands. *Playboy* featured Jayne every February from 1955 to 1958 and again in 1960. In 1957 *Playboy* said, ". . . Jayne has also developed more of an acting talent than might be expected from one of her proportions (40-21-32)." Jayne exposed more breast. Later in 1957 *Playboy* had a field day with the Sophia Loren–Jayne affair. Of Loren they said, "Loren is probably more beautiful than ever, but she reveals relatively little of that beauty to the public . . . For as starlets rise in the Hollywood heavens, becoming honest-to-gosh stars, they just seem to naturally shy away from all that sexy stuff that helped put them up there in the first place. This accompanied an early, bare-chested picture of Loren. About Jayne they said, "— the more stellar Jayne becomes, the greater the alacrity with which she divests herself of her duds. We applaud this as most refreshing. Jayne has no delusions about the cause of her popularity (a noble cause it is) and to deny or ignore it at this stage of the game apparently strikes her as the worst sort of snobbery." The smarmy insinuations should have made Jayne wince, but instead she went right on taking off her clothes.

In February 1958 *Playboy* ran "The Nude Jayne Mansfield." This year, they said, ". . . our vivacious valentine graciously graces our pages in the first figure studies she has ever allowed to appear in print. Jayne has posed for some pretty pulchritude-packed pictures in the past, but till now she has skirted the *au naturel*. This is, in fact, the very first time that a full-fledged star has posed so revealingly." In the pictures there is everything but pubic hair. Letters flowed in debating Jayne's anatomy. She was "the most perfect specimen of womanhood" and a "gourd-breasted, slack-jawed, slack-hipped broad with grotesquely protruding, gnarled, becorned feet . . ." *Playboy*, recapping in December 1958, ran a picture of Jayne in long rhinestone earrings and an open plaid shirt and wrote, " 'The Nude Jayne Mansfield' helped make that issue the biggest seller in *Playboy*'s history."

In 1960 *Playboy* revisited Jayne, remarking that "the number of filmic hopefuls who've been willing to strip to the buff in order to gain attention and give their careers a beginning boost has been, as they say, legion. Our Jayne, however, now that she's reached the top, continues to disrobe at the snap of a camera shutter wherever she may be." The pictures begin with a teen-age, brunette Jayne posing nude for an art class, go through the Loren pictures again and wind up with a sequence of Jayne in her Las Vegas *Too Hot to Handle* outfit, the net dress with the three sequin clusters.

In June 1963 the *Promises, Promises!* pictures appeared

○ ○ ○ ○ ○ ○ ○ ○ ○ ○ ○ ○ ○ ○ ○ ○ ○ ○ ○ ○ ○ ○ ○ ○ ○ ○ ○ ○ ○ ○ ○ ○ ○ ○ ○ ○ ○ ○ ○

under the title "The Nudest Jayne Mansfield." Jayne was wearing bikini panties, a towel or nothing. She rolled around in a bubble bath and on a pink bed pushing and pulling the sheets. *Playboy* said, "No capital in the world is more cunning at playing peekaboo with the human body (female) than our film capital. . . . The recent wave of 'nudie' movies, however, has injected a breath of fresh air upon the scene. Their unpretentious nakedness and wide public acceptance have helped push bodices down and hemlines up (to where they virtually vanish) in otherwise 'straight' productions.

"It is therefore fitting and proper that the trail from 'nudie' to 'straight' films be blazed by none other than the undisputed champion of in-the-altogether brinksmanship, Miss Jayne Mansfield. Jayne now proudly heads the scant list of authentic Hollywood heroines whose feats of baring-do go beyond the call of duty." The magazine was a sell-out at 2,000,000 copies. In New York copies were bootlegged for five and ten dollars.

In March 1964 *Playboy* reran a 1955 picture of Jayne. The next mention of her was in 1965 in an interview with the Beatles. Paul said, "She's a clot. But you won't print that anyway, of course, because *Playboy* is very pro-Mansfield. They think she's a rave. But she really is an old bag."

*Playboy* never did another feature on Jayne.

When *Playboy* went on the stand with "The Nudest Jayne Mansfield" Hugh Hefner was taken to the police station in Chicago and fined the standard obscenity fine of $200. He wrote in his new column, "The Playboy Philosophy," a series of articles dealing with the changing definitions of obscenity in America and with the attacks on Playboy Enterprises by Chicago authorities.

In his curious defense of the Mansfield pictures Hefner cites the fact that Noonan was playing her "hubby," that he was fully clothed and that he remained uninterested in

o o o o o o o o o o o o o o o o o o o o o o o o o o o o o o o o o o o o o o

her despite her thrashings.  The upshot of the sequence
has Jayne giving way to laughter and giving up as seduc-
tress.  Hefner says the pictures are not obscene because her
sexuality didn't triumph.  Farce isn't prurient.  "The pictures of Jayne in the June issue are, in our opinion, simply
candid photographs of a movie in the making."  *Playboy*
always had it both ways.  Hefner nobly quoted Mark
Twain.  " 'Man is merely and exclusively the Immodest
Animal, for he is the only one with a soiled mind, the only
one under the dominion of a false shame!"

Playboy's squirmy language seems evidence enough of
its own false shame, e.g., "Jayne has no delusions about
the cause of her popularity (a noble cause it is) . . . but till
now she has skirted the *au naturel* . . . Our Jayne . . . continues to disrobe at the snap of the shutter."  Their arch
euphemisms, possessive paternalism and runaway allitera-
tion fairly simper and blush.  Jayne could only be confused
by *Playboy*'s triple entendres and standards.  *Playboy*
courted her when she was young.  They wooed her to follow up Monroe's calendar shot.  For years Jayne was their
"primary" or "secondary sex feature."  Without being too
melodramatic it can be said that they seduced and aban-
doned her.  Jayne went along with *Playboy* in everything.
At their suggestion she posed for "The Nudest Jayne
Mansfield" and they never did a feature on her again.

Jayne wrote to Hefner:

> I have just finished reading the October installment of *The
> Playboy Philosophy*.  I am in complete accord that Jayne Mans-
> field per se is not the issue.  This is a matter of censorship, in
> that a few are trying to govern the tastes of many.  I strongly
> support you in your efforts to keep the press free, and in your
> championing each individual's right to make up his own
> mind.

The editors added this note:  "We are pleased that such an

authoritative source concurs in our belief that Jayne Mansfield is not obscene."

Jayne greedily fell on Hefner's freedom of speech argument. How, after all, can a woman entertain the idea that she is obscene? But his attitude, condescending and smug, was just as degrading as the censors'. Jayne had to defend herself against confusing and contrary positions — the pleasure she gave some, the outrage she provoked in others, the editors and readers who wanted more of it and the censors who wanted none of it. In the beginning she was saying, "I did it to buy milk for my baby." Later she didn't know the pictures were being taken and finally that she wasn't obscene. The culture wouldn't allow her to answer, as Ursula Andress did in 1969, a question about why she liked to be photographed nude. "Why do I do it? Because I'm beautiful." Jayne was always convinced that she was doing something wrong.

So Jayne and *Playboy* parted company. She became history for them as fast as the Edsel. They let her go and moved on to quote Paul McCartney to prove that they could be disloyal even to "the sexy stuff that helped put them up there in the first place."

Before Hefner started taking himself seriously, in 1959 when he began taking stands against strontium 90 and censorship, he and Jayne had both shared the belief that she was dirty. Hefner climbed in the sixties to great preachy heights, intoning that sex, nudity and *Playboy* were all in defense of separating church and state. He constructed long, boring essays arguing what the flower children already knew. Jayne was a bad memory of a preliberated period when he couldn't justify *Playboy* as moral uplift.

Shortly after the *Playboy* dispute, Jayne took on the Soviet Union. In Moscow that summer Jayne told Russian women, "I have preserved my appearance thanks to regular exercise with barbells, which has opened the door to being healthy, young and successful." *Soviet Culture* took out after Jayne as a symbol of a decadent and collapsing society. She is "a Philistine with a huge bust who has no need of acting talent." The Russians had done some faulty research. Her bathtub, they said, "which resembles a small swimming pool, says, 'I love Mickey' on the bottom."

Jayne corrected them. "Whatever NKVD man examined my home obviously mistook my pool for my bathtub. My pool has written on its bottom, 'I love you, Jaynie,' which was not self-inscribed. When I sit on my bathtub, I sit on nothing but myself."

Cimber coached Jayne to respond to the charge of Philistinism. "I must remind the Russians," she said, "that it was their great stage figure, Konstantin Stanislavsky, who said an actor's greatest success in the final analysis is his audience appeal.

"As far as my talent is concerned, I would be most happy to be invited by the Moscow Art Theater to appear there in one of my favorite plays, *The Sea Gull*, by Anton Chekhov and let them judge for themselves." Cimber says she'd never heard of Chekhov or *The Sea Gull*.

Mr. Blackwell hadn't stopped picking on Jayne. First he demanded that his credits be removed from *Promises, Promises!* for which he had designed Jayne's costumes. He put Jayne on his Worst Dressed List again, saying, "After appearing like a stuffed sausage for many years Jayne has resorted to the baby pink look — the baby doll shorties and darling pink bows for her multicolored hair, groomed not unlike the sweeping end of a broom. Has she in confusion borrowed her young daughter's wardrobe?"

In the fall of 1964 Jayne and Matt flew to Rome where Jayne made a quickie movie, more in the Mansfield than in the Fellini–De Sica vein. It was called *Primitive Love* and was a sort of travelogue with Jayne visiting nightclubs, judging beauty contests and going to a massage parlor. A movie released posthumously, *The Wild Wild World of Jayne Mansfield,* used some of the same footage and included Mickey touring the palace and police film of Jayne's fatal accident.

Cimber organized Jayne's career around TV and night-clubs. "Before me she wouldn't do TV or nightclubs. I made her do TV. CBS offered her a role on "Gilligan's Island" with a bigger part than Tina Louise has now. But the pay was too low, one thousand dollars a week for ten weeks' work. I turned it down."

Cimber describes Jayne's nightclub style. "She did an unrehearsed song and dance number. She'd do half an hour out in the audience. She'd introduce girls to guys, take material from the customers and use it. Her secret was that the women loved her. She was so sweet and so nice and they just loved her."

Cimber also had Jayne doing a lot of guest appearances on talk shows. He says she was in great demand by Barbara Walters, Johnny Carson and Jack Paar. Garson Kanin says that Jayne was responsible for Dick Cavett's getting his own program. Cavett had to stand in unexpectedly for Carson one night. His first guest was Jayne, and Cavett, intensely nervous but looking for the open shot, introduced her: "And here they are, Jayne Mansfield." Cimber says, "All the comedians wanted to work with her. Gleason is difficult but brilliant. He loved Jayne and would never say anything bad about her. We were always the first to go backstage when he was on. He said she had the best comic timing of any actress he'd worked with. She could set up a comedian to do a joke on her better than anyone else." That was the secret of her timing, that she set herself up to be humiliated by aggressive sexual humor.

Matt goes on. "I had an idea to put together a TV special with her great moments with Carson, Paar, Gleason, Hope

and the others.  The proceeds would go to the children.
But I figure they're well off and I'll wait.  Maybe in nineteen seventy-seven.  Carson thinks it's the greatest idea in
the world.''

A couple of Matt's ideas didn't pan out.  He tried unsuc-
cessfully to get Jayne ''a homey radio show called ''Life
With Jayne.''  It was to be, said Jayne, ''about the funny
things that happen to Jayne every day.''  He also tried
without success to get a part for her in a film called *The
Evasion* to be shot in Tokyo.

Jayne said, ''My career is moving in a sensitive direction.
I'm going to do a movie in which I portray three parts: a
prostitute, a cripple and a pregnant unmarried . . . I want
to make a big indentation on the world.''

The film which was going to move Jayne in a sensitive
direction was called *Single Room Furnished*.  It was released
in a few Florida drive-ins and the only person who liked it
was Walter Winchell.  Jayne had confused serious theater
with a cheap production, shabby costumes and an improb-
able story.  The author of the play is still suing Cimber and
the Mansfield estate for payment for the story.

In the summer of 1965, while Jayne was pregnant, she
and Matt toured Canada doing Cimber's rewritten version
of *Nature's Way* by Herman Wouk.  In Cimber's rendition
the heroine was pregnant.

Meanwhile Mickey was in danger in Rome.  On June 3,
1965, he reported that he was knifed and hit on the head in
his apartment there.  ''I tell you the truth, I'm lucky to be
alive.  I'm all mixed up and confused about this.  Who did
it?  I don't know.  It could be so many people.  But honestly I don't feel I've done anybody any harm.  I always try
to be nice to people.  I don't see why anybody would do
such a thing.''

Mickey's producer, Ralph Zucker, with whom Mickey
was working on a film called *The Crimson Executioner*, sug-

gested that a possible motive was jealousy over Hargitay's engagement to French actress Marie Vincente. "They were photographed a lot at the Cannes Film Festival. After the festival Mickey came back to Rome and Marie went to Paris. A few days ago she got in the mail a picture of her and Mickey taken from an Italian magazine. There was a big red lipstick kiss on the picture and a sentence written in bad English saying, 'He belongs to me. Leave him alone or I'll kill him.' " It was not for nothing that Mickey had been married to Jayne and a friend of Jim Byron's.

On October 18, 1965, Jayne gave birth to Anthony Richard Cimber at the Cedars of Lebanon Hospital. Cimber dates his troubles with Jayne from then. "We got along great until the child arrived. Then Jayne got very possessive of me and didn't want me to spend time with the kid. What she wanted for her kids was O.K., but I didn't want my son traveling all over the world. Now I don't know. Then I thought it was all her fault and blamed it all on her."

Cimber was appalled at the educational state of Jayne's children, particularly Jayne Marie. They took the fourteen-year-old to a convent school on Long Island where the nuns tested her and found her woefully deficient in all subjects. Matt says, "Mickey and Jayne never had a book in the house. I don't think those kids ever read a book all the way through. They never stayed in one school for more than a few months." Matt says that Jayne had Jayne Marie "combing her mother's hair and doing her fingernails instead of doing her homework."

Jayne's version was different. "I want to give my children the best that money and a loving heart can buy. I'm against the way American children are brought up; they blow their lives . . . They should be given a lot of responsibility. I'm a strong disciplinarian."

Jayne Marie said, "I admire my mother. She's so good,

so talented.  People look at her because she's so pretty . . .
She can make people laugh and cry.  She's like a sister to
me . . . She'll call me 'mother' and I'll call her 'Jayne.'  If I
do something wrong she'll punish me . . . but she only
spanks me when I really need it.  When I get older I'm
going to appreciate what she's done for me."

As far as education went, Jayne said, "I told Jaynie Marie
about sex on the way to dancing school, much the way a
father tells a son: Sex should be a pleasure, but you
shouldn't be promiscuous . . . When I was told about sex
first I laughed and then I cried . . . I couldn't see the point.
Fortunately, I changed."

Jayne and her daughter had a special, close relationship.
Jaynie Marie mothered her mother, organizing trips, packing and taking care of the money.  Jayne thought of the girl
as an adult yet wanted her to be a small child.  She dressed
her up as a little girl long after she'd become an adolescent.
Jayne loved her daughter but put her needs for admiration
and companionship before Jaynie Marie's childish concerns.

Jayne had been more or less on the wagon during the lat-
ter months of her pregnancy, but after the baby, Matt says,
"She went on a diet for six months of one cup of beef
bouillon, one bottle of bourbon and one bottle of champagne a day."

Matt, the most careful of men, doesn't drink.  Once
Jayne taunted him into drinking six martinis.  He was sick
and never did it again.  Jayne usually drank bourbon out
of Coke bottles and, according to Matt, used Jaynie Marie
as her bartender.  He wanted her to quit or slow down, but
she surrounded herself with drinking buddies to keep her
company.

In Florida Matt asked a doctor for a drug which, when
taken in conjunction with alcohol, makes the drinker sick
and disinterested in further drinking.  He says he plied

○ ○ ○ ○ ○ ○ ○ ○ ○ ○ ○ ○ ○ ○ ○ ○ ○ ○ ○ ○ ○ ○ ○ ○ ○ ○ ○ ○ ○ ○ ○ ○ ○ ○ ○ ○

Jayne's Coke bottled with what, for anyone else, would have been a sickening amount of the drug. It had no effect. The only time she wasn't drinking, Matt says, was when she was working. "She had fantastic discipline about everything except drinking." Even the separation of work and drink wasn't complete. In Tahoe Jayne got drunk on champagne just before show time. She stuck forks in her hair informing the producer that she was going on that way. He got Carol Burnett to fill in instead.

May Mann reports that Jayne always felt she loved Matt more than he loved her. Matt says it was a marriage of convenience for both of them. It may have been so, but Jayne used exactly the same language about Matt as she had about Mickey, Bomba, Sardelli and so on. She couldn't live without thinking she was in the throes of high drama and great passion. Otherwise it was a betrayal of everything she believed in, a total admission of her loss of innocence and corruption. The suspicion may have nagged at her that she did not love Matt as she professed. Certainly the suspicion lurked that he did not love her and, if one is to believe his testimony, he did not love Jayne. Her life was going into its last and saddest phase. She was making accommodations and compromises, lying to herself about what she was doing. The louder the inner voices got, trying to tell her what a mess everything was, the more she had to drown them out. So she drank.

In Cimber she found someone to run her. She miscalculated again, however, in assuming she would submit any more than she had submitted to Mickey's chest expansion. She fought back to preserve herself, at the moment when she most wanted to give herself up. Cimber, a self-described male supremacist, says, "I'll never get involved with another career woman." Jayne always hoped to lose herself in a man and failed. The control, the drive and the ambition which she had nurtured for years wouldn't stop.

Her little girl act represented a fantasy which she wouldn't allow herself to realize.  No one could father her for long.  So she and Matt fought bitterly over Jayne's Jayne.  Toward the end of 1965 Jayne said something which reflected the change in time over the previous decade but which also reflected the cynicism she was struggling with.  "As to loving someone you are not married to, I don't approve of affairs.  But if you have to have them, it's best to have them privately."

One of the activities to which Matt introduced Jayne was litigation.  Albert Zugsmith and the Famous Players Corporation sued Jayne, Matt and General Artists Corporation, an agency, for breach of contract.  Jayne had agreed to star in a movie to be shot in Turkey in the summer of 1965.  Matt and GAC had allegedly "maliciously and wrongfully induced her to break the contract."  The palace was attached, the suit and damages amounting to $382,000.  Zugsmith was still suing when Jayne died.  After Zugsmith, suits were slapped on Jayne like graffiti on the New York subways.

# Breaking Up Is Hard to Do

PART II

♥ ♥ ♥

MATT ARRANGED a deal with producer Richard Randall. Matt was to direct and Jayne was to star in a comedy by Rex Carlton called *The Rabbit Habit*. It did so badly out of town that instead of opening on Broadway in January 1966 Jayne opened at the Latin Quarter. She was making $11,000 a week and was a big success. Cimber's cousin Tony Bennett was playing nearby at the Copacabana. Matt says proudly, "Jayne had a line around the block waiting for her and Tony had about four people."

Jayne went on television talk shows three or four times a week, being a personality and talking up a picture she had made while she was pregnant. The film was called *The Fat Spy* and was an unfunny spoof on the James Bond movies with Jackie Leonard, Jordan Christopher and Phyllis Diller playing a counterspy. Matt produced a cheap, ghastly movie called *The Las Vegas Hillbillies* in which Jayne plays a star who aids two Appalachian dimwits to set up a country and western nightclub in Las Vegas.

But holding the marriage together became harder and harder. Matt says, "She could never relax, sit down on a Sunday evening, take her shoes off and watch TV."

In the subsequent custody fight over Tony, Matt testified that the family had gone to Baltimore in June. Jayne had come back to the hotel drunk at 3:00 A.M., waked Jaynie Marie up and had her make drinks. One night when Jayne was particularly angry, Matt said she cut off her daughter's hair. The girl denied this in court.

Matt charged that in July in New York Jayne hired something called a "registered homosexual" nurse to take care of the children. Matt protested and Jayne slapped him, whereupon he slapped her. This, he said, was the only time he ever laid an angry hand on Jayne. She accused him in court of beating her repeatedly. Matt now says, "Do I look like the kind of guy who would beat her up?" Jayne hired a policeman to prevent Matt from seeing his child. Jayne moved to another hotel where, Matt said, Mickey and journalist Jan Cremer moved into her suite.

Mickey had returned from Rome to "protect" Jayne. Jayne testified that Matt had made threats on Tony's life. Jayne and Mickey had a reunion dinner in New York with the four oldest children. "Jayne needs me now," said Mickey. "I never felt I wasn't married to her. I've never been out of love with her." Jayne announced that Mickey was going to South America with her. Cimber was still her manager, "but you're allowed to have friends," she said.

Jayne flew to Bogotá without Mickey and then to Caracas where she was going to the première of *The Fat Spy*. She had announced her separation from Matt on July 22, 1966. "We will still be together, for Matt is continuing as my manager. You know he is one of the best in the business. We are going to try hard to work out our problems but a legal separation seems the best answer right now." Almost immediately she filed for a divorce on the grounds of "extreme cruelty and grievous mental suffering."

Accompanying Jayne to South America was Salvatore

"Ted" Sifo, a friend of Matt's. Sifo was Cimber's witness in the custody suit and his testimony indicates that Jayne had an astonishingly energetic and varied sexual trip.

In Venezuela Jayne met and fell in love with twenty-year-old Douglas Olivares. Matt testified that while in Venezuela Jayne had called him and forced him to speak with Olivares. It was undoubtedly a conversation characterized by its brevity since Douglas spoke no English. Douglas, who was hardly dry behind the ears, had long eyelashes and short, curly hair. He referred to Jayne as "mi estrella [my star] baby face."

On her way home, Jayne had some trouble because the Venezuelans claimed she hadn't paid her exit taxes after earning money in their country. Olivares and Sifo pitched in to help out and Jayne made it home, bringing the radiant Douglas with her. Immediately, Cimber abducted ten-month-old Tony and took him to his mother's house in Huntington Beach. Jayne and Matt's agreement had been that Matt should have unlimited visiting privileges with Tony as long as he never took the child from the palace.

Cimber said he took Tony because Jayne was drunk with Douglas when she arrived at the airport. On the way home she insisted on stopping for more whiskey and then introduced Douglas to the children as their new father. Matt told Jayne to stop drinking. She refused unless he returned Tony. Matt arrived at the palace to discuss the matter and found fifteen people drunk, Jayne sitting on Olivares' lap and the kids serving drinks. Matt said he wouldn't bring Tony back.

It wasn't only the Venezuelans who thought Jayne owed them taxes. Jayne was into the IRS for $50,000, which she had to borrow from Matt. In September, she opened at the Fremont Hotel to earn some money. The Fremont is a downtown hotel in Las Vegas, not as glamorous as the Dunes or the Tropicana where Jayne used to play with

Mickey. With her she brought Douglas, who, she said, was acting as her recording secretary. Presumably for her Spanish correspondence.

Olivares was quickly displaced by Samuel Brody, a lawyer who was working with Jayne on her custody fight. Brody was an intense man, short with heavy features. Many considered him an intellectual and all were surprised about his relationship with Jayne. He had worked with Melvin Belli's firm and helped defend Jack Ruby. Belli said later, "He was a great lawyer and a helluva trial man. He was one of the sweetest guys I ever knew. How he got mixed up with Jayne I don't know, but his practice went to hell after he met her. He chased all around the world with her. She must've been a very romantic girl to have attracted a guy as sweet as Sam."

Stanley Cowan, Jayne's sometime agent, saw Jayne at the Fremont. She played the show to him, coming over and sitting in his lap afterward. She took Cowan upstairs to her suite where he met Brody. "I could see right away it was really something," says Cowan. "He was very much in love with her at the time." The entire suite was filled with Brody's presents, teddy bears, stuffed animals and dolls of all descriptions. "Brody had a hell of a practice, wife and kids. He really flipped over her."

After her four weeks at the Fremont, Jayne returned to Hollywood and got Tony back in a temporary settlement. Cimber was given the right to visit his son for one hour twice a week in the presence of a third party. When she left the courthouse with Sam she said she feared for the baby's life. "That's a stupid thing to say," said Matt. Brody looked menacing and said, "You'll never get him."

Sam took a proprietary interest in Jayne's affairs from the start and she encouraged him. He was an experienced and expensive laywer and she needed his services. The fight with Cimber was long and brutal, and Brody threw himself into it with imagination and fervor. Brody's love for Jayne was devouring. He had to have her and she sometimes let him think he could.

To relax Jayne and Brody flew north to attend the San Francisco Film Festival. After inviting Jayne, who arrived in a sideless dress, David Sacks, festival chairman, said, "She was not invited. She came by herself. She's not welcome. I finally approached her and said, 'Madame, I don't know how much a pound you are charging, but whatever it is I will pay it if you will leave.' I suppose it would be nice to have some sexy starlets at the film festival as they do at Cannes. In my opinion, Miss Mansfield does not meet the standard."

Jayne replied, "I don't know what Mr. Sacks is talking about, I never met the man." May Mann explained Jayne's wardrobe difficulties. Sam, in a fit of rage, poured Scotch all over Jayne's regular clothes, leaving Jayne with only costumes, that is, a spangle here and a sequin there. So, Jayne had to make do with a very skimpy dress. But, Jayne concluded, "Sideless is better than topless, isn't it?" She and Sam took off on a Canadian tour the next day.

When Jayne returned she and Sam were fighting most of the time. He was beating her up. Regularly pictures would appear in the papers of Jayne with black eyes, her face coated with pancake make-up to cover the damages. Jayne alternately submitted to and taunted Brody. He flew into a rage every time she mentioned another man, which she did frequently. She provoked him partly to keep him on his toes and partly because she saw his violence as a demonstration of love. She needed him badly as a lawyer but more importantly as someone who was holding things together for her just then.

It is the cross of guilt which dominating women must bear. It is unfeminine to know what you want and to go after it with all your energy. When she was beaten, Jayne

o o o o o o o o o o o o o o o o o o o o o o o o o o o o o o o o o o o o o o o o o

achieved a feeling, rare for her, of submission. She always defined ideal relations between men and women as woman's subordination to a strong, wise man. Things had never worked out that way for Jayne in either her marriages or her affairs. She refused to know her own strength. Consequently, she felt that she'd missed out on the real romantic experience. She had tasted it in the beginning with Mickey, but it had only worked when she was suspending her critical faculties. The minute she replaced her fantasies with reality, she realized that she was tougher and more ambitious than Mickey and that her ambition was as important to her, or more so, than he was. But that was an intolerable admission and made her feel like an unnatural woman. She started searching for a ruler, not a partner. Bomba was going to be her Carlo Ponti, Cimber her Arthur Miller. She didn't abandon romance but tried to refurbish it or give it life in booze and brutality.

Brody's intense possessiveness acted as cement in Jayne's life. She had never enjoyed being free, and never stayed single for long. Her need for attention and reassurance was at an all-time high. Brody was ideal for her purposes. He never took his eyes off Jayne. He had to possess her in a total way. The escalating violence with which he pursued her kept her excited and frightened, which was as good as being in love. They executed that tormented stalemate: "Can't live with 'em, can't live without 'em."

At the end of November, Jayne and Sam, the children, Dr. Murray Banks, a psychologist and friend of Jayne's, and several journalists including May Mann went to Thousand Oaks, a community in the San Fernando Valley where Jayne was making a personal appearance at Jungleland, a zoo. Jayne was posing, adjusting Miklos' tie, when a large and presumably tame lion grabbed six-year-old Zoltan.

The lion slashed the little boy's cheek and gave him a skull fracture. The lion was holding Zoltan between its teeth when the zoo manager pulled apart its jaws and Banks extracted the boy.

May Mann told reporters that Jayne "screamed and screamed and screamed." When she had calmed down a little, she went to the Conejo Valley Community Hospital. Five neurosurgeons worked all day on Zoltan's skull. They sewed up the gash and put particles of bone back in place in the skull, relieving the pressure on his brain. Jayne's "spokesman" told the press that Jayne had taken a room in the hospital to wait until Zoltan's recovery was no longer in question. The spokesman was Stanley Cowan, who had called Jayne the night of the accident. She was at home gathering up some clothes for her stay at the hospital. Cowan drove to the hospital and met her there. "She was completely beside herself. Mickey was in Rome. Jayne put a call through and he said he'd be back as soon as possible."

Jayne told Cowan to notify the papers and get a press report out every day. It was, he said, "one of the greatest publicity setups in the world."

On November 30, five days after the accident, Mickey flew back from Rome where he had been shooting another epic. "Zoltan," he announced, "was the victim of his own courage for not having fear of anything. Just to think he is only six years old. He is a wonderful boy, good and generous. I can't wait to be by his side because I am very worried." By this time the doctors felt that Zoltan was making good progress.

Jayne, meanwhile, had been thrown out of the hospital because she and Sam were drinking and fighting all over the place. They were, according to one witness, "drinking and swinging at each other up and down the hospital corridors at 1:00 A.M." Their behavior upset the staff and patients and Jayne was asked to leave. Cowan's release read, "Miss Mansfield yesterday was not permitted to visit her son at Conejo Valley Community Hospital because she was stricken with a virus pneumonia and her temperature rose to 103 degrees."

"I'm not going into a hospital for myself because if Zoltan's condition changes I wouldn't be able to rush to his side." At this point, Zoltan developed spinal meningitis and the doctors again considered his condition critical.

Soon, however, Zoltan rallied and Jayne told Cowan that the hospital was going to let her bring him home for Christmas. "Wonderful," he said, "I'll get the story in the papers."

Jayne said, "Call a press conference at home on Christmas morning."

"It won't work. No one will show."

"Yes, they'll come for me."

Cowan remembers, "It was a weekend. I called reporters apologetically, invited them to a press conference for the baby's arrival home. I promised a lot of refreshments."

He was to meet Jayne and Brody at the palace at ten o'clock Christmas morning, drive out to the hospital with them and come home with Zoltan. "I got there at ten and Jayne Marie said, 'Mother's not up yet, but I'll wake her.' Jayne called down that she wouldn't be long. I was really mad and yelled at her about how she made me get there at ten. Sam walked out of her room in the middle of my speech. I realized we won't get off till noon, at least. So, I got the maid to order a lot of food and liquor. Finally we leave to go to the hospital. When we got there I called the house to see how many press were there and there were ten. I thought that was fine and said we'd be there in a half an hour to forty-five minutes. When we got back there was no place to park. There were thirty-five or forty reporters. They loved her. The Christmas tree was up and they all took pictures of the baby."

It was a successful holiday. The kids had a good time and there were lots of presents. Zoltan got special treatment, of course, as well as a robot, a bat, baseballs, a kickstand for his bike and plenty of other things. Jayne was happy to have Zoltan home and happy to have been on the front page for three weeks.

She wasn't callous about Zoltan's injury. She was terribly upset, but it was natural for her to think of telling the press. She was accustomed to reading about herself and she knew the public would be interested. The news was made and Jayne wasn't going to suppress it. She had worked for years to become news and her reward was having the press cooperate with her. There were pictures of Jayne and Zoltan, Jayne, Sam and Jayne, Mickey and Jayne and Zoltan, Jayne and Zoltan on the front pages of newspapers all across the country. Jayne's grief was transcontinental.

Over the years publicity had had an effect on Jayne's perceptions. She ceased to recognize a difference between public and private. Her love affairs and her children were news. Her unhappiness about Zoltan wasn't entirely real to her until she saw it in print. She had become the person she and the newsmen had created. She depended upon seeing herself as a way of confirming who she was.

She no longer distinguished between her own life and her life as news. She liked May Mann, Earl Wilson, Joe Hyams and countless other reporters and columnists. Talking to them was talking to friends. Jayne instinctively called Louella Parsons whenever anything happened to her. She had come to a point where she simply didn't know on stage from off.

Two examples illustrate this. She and Mickey did an interview with *Photoplay* in 1963. The interviewer, Jim Hoffman, asked Mickey about their marital status. Mickey said they usually went to the Wayfarers' Chapel every year to repeat their wedding vows. This year they had not. Mickey turned to Jayne and said, "Jaynie, will you marry me?" Jayne blushed and her eyes filled up with tears.

Toward the very end of her life Jayne was on a TV talk show with Mickey in the midwest. Mickey was gaunt, having suffered from ulcers and given up body building. Jayne looked at him and said that she was sorry for all the trouble she'd given him, that she wished she had been nicer. Jayne had forgotten that she was on camera or, rather, it made no difference to her.

Also, Jayne misjudged the change in the times. Early on she had censored her press so that she came out looking like the girl who couldn't help it. She had spent the first years of her career talking up a restrictive code of ethics and had kept her private, sexual life relatively quiet. Gradually she began to feel that what had been private could now be tolerated publicly. She could live with Sam and give interviews about the time she was raped as a teen-ager and it would be acceptable. But the sixties could not absorb Jayne, nor did she know what the period meant. The new morality made her uncomfortable, whereas the double standards of the previous decade made perfect sense. She was more at home with an innuendo and a wink than with the bluntness of the kids. She saw herself as a dispenser of sexual favors, not an equal member of a sexual or social union. She couldn't act spontaneously, deprived of the ritual mating dances she had learned as a girl. Her behavior was as rigid as a No player's. She was to tease and be chased. More than that she didn't know. She never knew why she had become bad news. As Cowan said of her, "She was her own worst enemy."

So, although Jayne began to give up catering to the sensibilities of the lady from Dubuque, she went on catering to the lady's husband.  She played in unprepossessing clubs in her skimpy costumes, sitting on the laps of old men who thought she was a sexy piece and stuffed dollars down her bosom.

# *1967*

♥ ♥ ♥

THE WOMEN'S MOVEMENT tries to encompass all women, but Jayne is hard on a feminist. Karen Lindsey wrote an "Elegy for Jayne Mansfield, July 1967."

> she was a
> sunday news centerfold
> bosoms thrust toward subway-
> rush men leaning on the
> legs of pretty secretaries
> always a bleeding
> divorce or a beaten child,
> she had a pink voice, and lived in a pink house.
> no hints of self
> cringing away from sticky headlines
> or an art groping beyond
> barebreasted titters
>
> we used to have fun laughing at her,
> when she lost her head, the joke turned sick.*

* *Sisterhood Is Powerful*, ed., Robin Morgan (New York: Random House, 1970), p. 496.

○ ○ ○ ○ ○ ○ ○ ○ ○ ○ ○ ○.○ ○ ○ ○ ○ ○ ○ ○ ○ ○ ○ ○ ○ ○ ○ ○ ○ ○ ○ ○ ○ ○ ○ ○ ○ ○

By making herself sexually outrageous, Jayne made it hard for sober, serious-minded feminists to incorporate her in the greater sisterhood. But Jayne was a woman and a public figure and she had an important place in women's time. In a negative sense she was a model of how not to be. Somebody had to prove that being a sex symbol was a dubious occupation. The Monroe mythology grows every day, and it almost seems as if her life were desirable. With Jayne there is no room for doubt. And the awful things in her life were a direct result of wanting to be "America's pinup girl" all her life.

Jayne suffered from the sexual stereotype forced on a woman with a forty-inch bust. There was nothing else she could be but sexy, and there was no way anyone could respond to her but sexually. She was at the mercy of men's approval. She suffered from a host of cultural myths about romance and weak, childish women needing strong, powerful men. The older Jayne got the younger she dressed and talked, as if only through infantilism could she be treated like a real woman, condescended to, protected, swept off her feet. Jayne suffered from being an unusually strong and courageous woman in a society which prefers its women cowardly and undecided. The baby talk and stuffed animals happened in the sixties. In the fifties Jayne was merely trying to suggest brainlessness. Her private relationships changed too. Her first two marriages had been with equals, when Jayne was looking for love and sex and fun and companionship. Then her demands on men grew. They had to be wiser and more powerful than she. She began sliding backward into dependency as her career failed her.

Jayne dealt with the necessity to be girlish in a characteristically straightforward way. If the country wanted its women girlish, she'd be so girlish that everyone would gag on the word. Jayne's career failed because of the timing —

the enormous social change which put Jayne out of an act. She is a measure of how much the society changed in her lifetime. She stayed essentially the same while women discarded one by one the tricks and ploys she demonstrated. The tease became obsolete, the obvious come-on was gone, the little girl was becoming less desirable as women were allowed to mature sexually. Style is a mirror of attitudes and Jayne's style became vulgar and unseemly when it had once been acceptable and fun.

Jayne had determination, self-confidence, self-reliance and an overwhelming desire to succeed. She applied these traits to a career based on an exploited image of women. By exploiting that image, Jayne was eaten up by the culture. But in her own canny way, Jayne got back at society. When Jayne realized, in the sixties, that she wasn't going to be the celestial blond sex goddess of all time, she made sure that no one else would either. When Jayne died that particular American dream died too.

In some ways Jayne was a very liberated woman if liberation means pouring your energies into a goal outside the home. She gave her motherly and wifely responsibilities a lick and a promise and plunged on with her career. Jayne never cooked or sewed, or waited for her husband to come home from a hard day at the office, or organized a coffee klatsch, or gave a Tupperware party, or entertained the boss and his wife or drove the kids to school in a paneled station wagon. She had a dizzy, frenetic life of her own making.

Like everyone who is complicated, Jayne makes bad ideology. She cannot, however, be blamed for the character she constructed. She took the materials at hand and turned them into an idea. That idea finally exceeded the bounds of good taste and Jayne became a cultural no-no because she mocked the character she had been allowed to project. She didn't keep her place or her part of the bargain. She let her imagination and sense of the ridiculous take her too far in a caricature of the sexy woman. She was intolerable when she wasn't serious about sex.

Jayne's great misfortune was to be a woman who couldn't live without male attention and approval, a woman for whom nothing was ever enough. Her hunger carried her to extremes of exhibitionism which proved counterproductive, turning off the men whom subtlety might have won. But she couldn't control her need.

Jayne was a sex-object lesson. She demonstrated how and why to do it, and what the price is. Ideology aside, she was original, honest, funny and hardworking. It wasn't until her style soured that she stopped to worry, and it wasn't until then that she stopped having fun. The damage society did to Jayne by focusing on her breasts was less painful, ultimately, than the loss she felt when she became an anachronism. Maturation was long overdue and Jayne was a casualty of the times like an Uncle Tom or Hubert Humphrey.

In January Jayne and Brody, always happy to litigate, sued Jungleland for negligence. They asked a million in punitive damages, $500,000 in general damages for Zoltan and $100,000 for Jayne's loss of earnings and worry.

After filing suit Jayne and Sam took off for the Far East. The quotes came back as if it were 1957. Bangkok: "American men are in kindergarten, European men are postgraduates, but Asian men — they are the best." After sampling Vietnam, Jayne and Brody started fighting and came home early.

Sam was busy concocting schemes for Jayne's future. He and Cowan conferred. Brody wanted to incorporate Jayne, have her do her own independent movies and merchandise her own line of clothes and cosmetics. Brody said, "We have to make a trip, but we'll talk about it when we're

o o o o o o o o o o o o o o o o o o o o o o o o o o o o o o o o o o o o o o

back." They didn't talk about it again because Jayne was, says Cowan, "methodical with a dollar. She felt people should give her a good deal because she was who she was. Through Brody she offered me practically nothing. I told her that if she wanted a favor I'd do it. But if she wanted to talk business then we should talk business." Jayne hadn't learned anything from her experience with Jim Byron.

Jayne was drinking more and behaving peculiarly. Matt Cimber was then spending time with Christy Hanak, the liquor heiress whom he later married. He was with her one night at a private club in Beverly Hills when Jayne drove up and sent a message to Matt saying, "I've got to see you." Matt came out to the car. "She was in the bag," he remembers. "You have to come back with me," she said. "I need to talk to you. Please come back with me to the house tonight." He said, "Tomorrow. You're drunk. Call me tomorrow." She insisted and he got in the car to talk.

Jayne drove to the intersection of Rodeo and Sunset, took the keys, got out of the car and ran across the junction to the Beverly Hills Hotel. Matt waited in the car for a while, then walked to the hotel. Jayne was on the phone talking to Sam. "He was telling her what to do." Matt went back to the car, which was surrounded by police. Jayne had called them and accused Matt of bothering her. They had seen Jayne drunk before and drove Matt back to the club with no comment.

Jayne and Sam were plotting ways to convince Judge Allen Lynch to give Tony to Jayne and win punitive damages from Matt. Matt, on the other hand, was cooking up ideas to prove that Jayne was an unfit mother. All three dreamed up large and small persecutions. Matt says Jayne and Sam used to follow him around from restaurant to restaurant. He customarily ate in a French spot in Beverly

o o o o o o o o o o o o o o o o o o o o o o o o o o o o o o o o o o o

Hills where Jayne and Sam never came. One night they appeared and came back every night, pretending not to notice Matt and making a lot of noise. Finally, after being forced out of his favorite restaurant, Matt was revenged. Brody racked up an enormous bill and asked the headwaiter to discount it for him one night because he was short of money. Sam and Jayne never ate there again.

Meanwhile, Beverly Brody, Sam's wife and the mother of their two children, thrust herself into the skirmish. She was then thirty-six and had been confined to a wheelchair because of multiple sclerosis. She sued Sam in July 1966 for $6000 a month in alimony and child support. She told reporters in February 1967 that "Miss Mansfield has telephoned me on a number of occasions and has very freely discussed with me her current love affair with my husband. The children of Jayne Mansfield have also witnessed the fact that she and my husband have occupied the same bed in the Jayne Mansfield home on a number of occasions." Mrs. Brody said that Jayne had told her that Sam had struck her on the mouth and that it took three stitches to close her lip.

A few days later, in Mrs. Brody's court actions against her husband, her lawyer called Jayne a "brazen and arrogant" woman. Beverly accused Jayne of being the forty-first woman with whom Sam had committed adultery. Mrs. Brody went on to say that Jayne and Sam had committed adultery not only in the United States, but also in Mexico, Canada and Japan. Sam said the complaint was only brought to harass him and force a property settlement with Mrs. Brody.

Jayne retorted that the accusations of adultery were "unfounded and ridiculous. Mr. Brody is my friend as well as my barrister. I deny the charge entirely. I'm very sorry this poor woman thinks otherwise. He's just a friend — and I have many friends."

Not to be upstaged, Jayne brought suit against Matt and Mrs. Brody for $60,000 in damages, charging that they had been harassing her day and night with phone calls. Her suit was a "complaint for interference with mental and emotional tranquillity" in which she stated that Mrs. Brody and Cimber had threatened her life and promised "unwarranted legal actions" in the phone calls. Jayne claimed there were twenty or thirty calls a day, that she was called "vile and abusive names." She wanted $10,000 to compensate for her "great mental anguish, mortification, humiliation and shame" and $50,000 punitive damages because the calls had been malicious. Informally, Jayne said she was bringing the action mainly to protect her children who were "not used to filth and profanity but loving care."

Beverly struck back. She asked the court to prohibit Jayne from associating with her children, Keith, nine, and Elizabeth, three, "Because of Jayne Mansfield's attitude about commonly accepted standards of decency and conduct, I believe our children would be endangered by permitting them to be in her presence."

Two weeks later, on March 28, Jayne filed suit against Matt for $45,000 for assault and battery. She said he used his "fists and mouth" to beat and bite her on the face and chest. She claimed that he attacked her four times in April 1966, rendering her unable to work. Cimber "kicked and stomped" and bit her "about the face and body in a fit of rage," the suit claimed.

With all suits pending, Jayne was given temporary custody of Tony. She, Sam and the baby left for England at the end of March, arriving at Heathrow March 24. Jayne was carrying Tony, and Sam was carrying Momsicle and Popsicle, two of Jayne's Chihuahuas. Sam was wearing Jayne's leopard-skin coat around his shoulders to conceal the dogs, but London customs officials found them and quarantined them. Jayne was, Brody said, "heartbroken.

○ ○ ○ ○ ○ ○ ○ ○ ○ ○ ○ ○ ○ ○ ○ ○ ○ ○ ○ ○ ○ ○ ○ ○ ○ ○ ○ ○ ○ ○ ○ ○ ○ ○ ○ ○ ○ ○ ○ ○ ○ ○

She is very fond of animals. She has forty of them at home in Los Angeles."

Like a flash Jayne went out and bought two new Chihuahuas from Mrs. Hillary Harmer of Surrey. When Mrs. Harmar respectfully asked for payment, Jayne replied:

> Thank you very much for your letter, inquiring after my little treasures. They took to me immediately like a mother, and sit on my lap constantly.
>
> Something unfortunate happened last night. When one of the gendarmes came into my dressing room, Precious Jewel leaped out of my lap onto the floor, in order to protect me. Suddenly she started limping. She broke her little leg. We immediately called for a Veterinary Surgeon, who placed a temporary bandage. This morning the leg was put in plaster. This has to stay for 2–3 weeks. But as usual both, she and Emerald are sitting in my lap, enjoying theirselves.
>
> With kindest regards,
>
> Affectionately,
>
> JAYNE MANSFIELD

Jayne never paid Mrs. Harmar, who is still trying to get payment from the estate.

Three weeks later Brody was fined $140 for trying to bring the dogs into England illegally. In the interim Jayne had been seeing the sights. She visited Parliament wearing a snug, blue and white minidress with a deep neck. Her escort was a Tory M.P. from Yorkshire, thirty-six-year-old Tim Kitson. Jayne expressed great enthusiasm for Edward Heath. "I just love that great big smile of his. Is it really true that he's a bachelor? I really go big for him. I wonder if he knows I'll be divorced soon. Someone said he had stayed a bachelor because he's never been lucky enough to meet a girl like me." Jayne had asparagus soup and ravioli with Kitson. Of Parliament at work, Jayne said, "I was very impressed by everything. I love all the pomp and ceremony, I sure did enjoy meeting all those lovely Whips."

Sam, meanwhile, had proposed to Jayne. "Jayne is a good mother, a good cook, highly provocative and very intelligent. She has an IQ of one hundred and sixty-three. And that's enough to make any man a super wife. Also our divorces come through at the same time in July. That means we can marry then."

Jayne said, "Sam's a marvelous man and I love him. We've been through thick and thin together. You can draw your own conclusions about whether I am going to accept."

Just a few days later Jayne announced, "I've been sacked." Jayne had a seven-week contract with Don Arden of Contemporary Records, who was promoting her club tour. After two weeks he fired her. His reasons were that she was always late, arrived in street clothes because she had forgotten her costume and had badly bruised legs. David Jacobs, Contemporary Records' lawyer, said they would sue Jayne for breach of contract. "Disfiguring black and blue marks from her knees up make it impossible to wear miniskirts called for in performances."

Jayne was "shocked and amazed by the ludicrous accusations." She admitted to being late for a couple of appearances, "but it was not my fault. The audiences loved me. I thought I was doing great. Business has been booming at the clubs and getting better every night. I've not been paid a penny under my contract. I'm not working unless I get paid."

Brody said, "So far she hasn't got a penny. Business was booming and I went to Don Arden to ask him for her first week's salary due to her. He then sent a telegram terminating the whole contract."

Arden counterattacked. "The reason she has not been

○ ○ ○ ○ ○ ○ ○ ○ ○ ○ ○ ○ ○ ○ ○ ○ ○ ○ ○ ○ ○ ○ ○ ○ ○ ○ ○ ○ ○ ○ ○ ○ ○ ○ ○ ○ ○ ○ ○ ○

paid any salary is because she has been charging all her expenses to my company. Because I am not in possession of all of them, I am unable to know exactly what to deduct from her salary. She will be paid what balance is due her so far."

As soon as she was canned, two other club owners stepped in to hire Jayne. She signed a contract for $11,200 a week, $2800 more than Arden had offered her, to play in Yorkshire at the Variety Club. The arrangement included a chauffeur-driven Rolls Royce, a hairdresser, a nurse for Tony and accommodations in luxury hotels.

Jayne, who had been pursued by singer Engelbert Humperdinck, threw him over when she met Allan Welles, a wealthy thirty-four-year-old club owner. Welles was a departure from Jayne's swarthy phase, resembling an undernourished Mickey. He and Jayne drove around in his Bentley and Jayne vowed that she loved him passionately. Three days before she had announced her engagement to Brody. Sam was beside himself. At a going-away party for Jayne, Welles and Brody had words. Allan pushed Brody into a passing tray of champagne glasses. A guest who tried to break up the spat found himself sitting on an enormous cake which had once read "Farewell to Jayne, Love from Allan." Jayne was taken away weeping.

Brody and Jayne patched it up and went on to Ireland. The Catholic diocese got Jayne thrown out of the Rose of Tralee Festival. Monsignor John Lane, the dean of the diocese, said, "It is my unpleasant duty to condemn in the strongest possible terms an entertainment that is taking place in Tralee this evening . . . This woman boasts that the New York critics said of her that she sold sex better than any performer in the world. 'As far as I'm concerned,' she says, 'I am a sexy entertainer.'" Jayne terminated her Irish tour.

Brody and Jayne had another brawl. Jayne wept for the

three days he spent in the United States. Cimber thinks that Brody and Nelson Sardelli were the only two men who ever really loved Jayne. If one judges love by the strength of the need and the ability to inflict injury, then Brody qualifies as a first-rate lover. Jayne was a purist and demanded exclusive devotion. She knew that Sam wasn't just devoted, he was obsessed. She lived at an exhausting emotional speed with him, was afraid of him, but he never bored her. Their relationship makes real neurotic sense when seen as part of a progression from adolescent romance to mature desperation.

Their next exploit was a trip to Stockholm where, as Jayne put it, "I made more money than Sammy Davis." That was the good news. The rest was drunken fights, jealousy and scenes. Jayne and Sam had an argument with a black guest at the Afroskandia Club. Blows were exchanged and Jayne wound up on the floor in a highly undignified sprawl, revealing what she had always said, that she wore no underclothes. The next night Jayne had to stay with a young man in a hospital because he slashed his wrists when she wouldn't go out with him. Recounting other misfortunes, Jayne said, "In Germany I sprained my back. The sink in my dressing room fell on my head." She giggled. On their way to Stockholm, Jayne and Brody lost their wardrobes, hers worth some $14,000. Brody got to sue the airline as well as Don Arden for the truncated nightclub tour.

Jayne was not looking forward to going home. She was afraid of Cimber and litigation was on her mind. "I'm frightened," she said. The only person she was looking forward to seeing was Mickey. "He is a wonderful friend. He'll testify for me at the divorce trial." She took a memento with her, a Rolls Royce. "It cost thirty-four thousand dollars." Her parting thoughts were, "I've thought of becoming a British citizen. It's so chic here. I want my children to go to school here and get a British accent."

Jayne and Sam arrived home to nothing but trouble. To gird herself, Jayne decided to convert to Judaism and marry Brody. "I've had some serious talks about it with Rabbi Nussbaum who converted Elizabeth Taylor and Sammy Davis."

Jayne Marie turned up at the West Los Angeles Police Station two weeks after her mother's arrival home. She was covered with bruises and welts and said Sam had beaten her, at her mother's urging, with his leather belt. She said that they had left her in a locked room under guard and that Brody had forced Jayne Marie to sign false affidavits for her mother on several occasions.

She showed up at the police station with Bernard Cohen, who was, oddly enough, Cimber's lawyer. She was armed with photographs of her injuries and bruises. She had had these photographs taken at her uncle Bill Pigue's house. Pigue was then on the city desk of the Los Angeles *Herald-Examiner*, and was actually Paul Mansfield's uncle, but had become a friend of Jayne's and had supported her to quite a lot of free publicity over the years. A precise man, Pigue charged Jayne's estate later for $3.38 for "film and flash bulbs to photograph bruises on ward's body" and another $2.40 for "prints of color photos of bruises." Pigue got in touch with Cohen, who, after the photography, took the girl to the police station. She said she wanted sanctuary and was placed in McLaren Juvenile Hall where she slept and ate well, required no medical treatments and got along well with the other inmates.

Brody said, "All of what she allegedly told the police is false. The girl has an emotional problem that causes her to react radically to discipline. We have documents and witnesses to attest to this." Jayne and Brody tried to see the girl during the few days she was there, but she refused. She wanted to go and live with the Pigues.

Jayne and Brody had to make sure they could settle the Jaynie Marie affair quietly or, they felt, their careers would be ruined. Jayne had just won her struggle with Cimber for Tony. Brody was particularly proud. "He [Judge Lynch] didn't say Jayne was a good mother. He didn't say she was a great mother. He said she was the greatest mother he'd ever seen." Now Jayne had to prove that premise all over again.

The Pigues sued for custody of Jayne Marie. Jayne opposed the suit on the grounds that Jayne Marie was no relative of theirs since Paul Mansfield, Pigue's nephew, had not been Jayne Marie's father. Instead, she told the courtroom, she had been raped by a gas station attendant from Dallas at the age of fourteen. She had chosen Paul Mansfield as a husband, instead of "Inky," the gas station attendant, "In the interests of the baby." One can imagine Brody's mind busy working up stories for Jayne.

She went on to say that Jayne Marie was being punished for having a naked boy in her closet and trying to introduce him to her mother, assuming that Jayne would find him attractive. Jayne was appalled. Jayne had allowed herself to think that she and her daughter were friends, but it was not so. Jayne, by asking Jayne Marie to do what she was told and not what she observed, had destroyed her daughter's confidence in her. Jayne Marie, as bartender, wardrobe mistress, hairdresser and personal maid, naturally considered herself her mother's contemporary. Jayne's reliance on the girl supported that conclusion.

Furthermore, Jayne Marie was in the position of growing older while her mother grew younger. Jayne had started out seventeen years older than her daughter, but the gap was down to fourteen by 1967. Jayne felt the need of mothering herself and taught her oldest to be a young

○ ○ ○ ○ ○ ○ ○ ○ ○ ○ ○ ○ ○ ○ ○ ○ ○ ○ ○ ○ ○ ○ ○ ○ ○ ○ ○ ○ ○ ○ ○ ○ ○ ○ ○ ○ ○ ○ ○

mother. Jayne Marie grew tired of the responsibility and angry at her mother for forcing it on her.

Jayne was willing to act as if she and her daughter were friends, but the things they shared were strictly limited and did not, in Jayne's assessment of the situation, include men. Jayne Marie knew the boundaries of her mock friendship with her mother and deliberately crossed them. Jayne mustered all her decaying authority when equality proved to be a sham.

It was virtually impossible for Jayne to admit that her child was a young woman, old enough to take care of herself, old enough to judge Jayne with a clear mind, but most of all, old enough and young enough to compete with her mother in sexual games. At sixteen Jayne Marie was a dark-haired, dark-eyed, pretty girl who had dropped much of her baby fat and adopted a rather sultry look. Her eyes were a little smaller than her mother's and her teeth weren't as dazzling, but she had dramatic coloring and, of course, youth.

It had been tricky for Jayne bobbing and weaving through all those roles: wife, mother, career woman, sex goddess. Hard as she tried to keep her lives separate, she mixed them up. Jayne Marie couldn't help but respond with confusion. She knew that her mother had unusual habits and unusual friends and that her behavior should have indicated great license if Jaynie Marie could judge by example. But just as Jayne didn't want her kids seeing *Promises, Promises!*, she didn't want them behaving like her. She punished Jaynie Marie in part for her own guilt.

Jayne Marie, by emulating Jayne, did exactly the wrong thing and it angered and confused her. It wasn't fair to be made to pay for doing the very thing she had learned from her mother. By the same token she was punishing Jayne for her contradictory behavior. And she was flaunting her adolescent sexuality.

Jayne was hurt, and not just because she thought the possibility of criminal charges would jeopardize her career. She loved her daughter but couldn't see that Jaynie Marie was crying out for understanding and attention. She had relied on her daughter as an ally too long. The girl had seen things way beyond her age and experience. She had accepted responsibilities in exchange for a close, special relationship with her mother. But just then she needed understanding more than chores. A pliable child, she was growing into an intractable, directionless and resentful adolescent. The most obvious method for calling attention to herself, her loneliness and despair at being a child–grown-up, was the same method her mother had always used.

The Pigues and Jayne Marie did not bring criminal charges against Brody and Jayne. The girl was, however, sent to live with the Pigues in Huntington Beach. Sam and Jayne went back to business. Brody considered the possibility of a five-minute daily TV show in which Jayne would hand out "naive but serious" advice on sex and love.

On a Monday morning in the middle of June, Sam drove into another car at the intersection of Sunset and Whittier in Beverly Hills. Jayne was not hurt, while Brody broke an elbow, a leg, a thumb and cracked two teeth. He was in two casts. "She must have been in the bag," said Cimber. "She never got up that early." Cimber was driving back from the Valley with Ted Sifo. He had been at a meeting with his lawyer and a judge when he heard the news. Shortly afterward in the car, he and Sifo heard that Brody and Jayne had put out a warrant for Cimber's arrest for attempted murder. The charges were dropped almost immediately, but Cimber had the satisfaction of knowing that Brody had done something uniquely stupid and that Cimber's alibi was unquestionable.

Less than a week later Jayne and Sam packed up and took off for Biloxi, Mississippi, where Jayne was playing at

o o o o o o o o o o o o o o o o o o o o o o o o o o o o o o o o o o o o o o o

the Gus Stevens Supper Club. Jayne took Mickey, Zoltan
and Maria, but, according to court orders, Tony stayed
home. Jayne was tired of being on the go. "I dream of the
day when I can stay home and have a little time like other
people to do things I like to do. I want to be just a woman,
not a breadwinner, but I have to keep working so the
money will come in to support my children."

The children weren't so much a drain as Sam. To be
sure, he was doing all her legal work free, but he was also
running up gigantic bills, like $14,000 for new plumbing
installations in the palace. Jayne was hardly a check-grab-
ber, but she knew she'd have to reckon with Sam's extrava-
gances sometime.

So, the more-or-less family went to Biloxi. Jayne opened
at Stevens' to an enthusiastic crowd. On the night of June
28 she finished a little early because she had to drive to
New Orleans to appear on a TV talk show in the morning.
She piled the kids and baggage into the back seat while
she, Brody and his casts and Ronald Harrison, the nine-
teen-year-old club driver, got in front.

Brody was sitting in the middle, Jayne in a blue mini-
dress and boots on his right. She was wearing her hair
long and straight with false eyelashes, heavy eye make-up
and thick pale lipstick. She looked pouchy and strained
from too much alcohol. The children were playing in the
front seat before Jayne told them to get in the back and lie
down. It was well past midnight and they were very tired.
They lay down on the floor in the back seat of the 1966
Buick. Harrison was driving along a slick treacherous section of Route 90. Some distance ahead Harrison saw a
large cloud coming from a slow-moving mosquito-spraying
machine. As Harrison drew closer, he slowed down and
drove into the fog. He couldn't see the trailer truck in
front of him and at 2:25 A.M., the Buick ran right under it.
The top of the car was peeled off like the top of a sardine

○ ○ ○ ○ ○ ○ ○ ○ ○ ○ ○ ○ ○ ○ ○ ○ ○ ○ ○ ○ ○ ○ ○ ○ ○ ○ ○ ○ ○ ○ ○ ○ ○ ○ ○ ○ ○ ○

can.  Harrison and Brody were thrown out and killed. Jayne was decapitated before her body flew out of the car. On the death certificate her injuries were given as "crushed skull with avulsion of cranium and brain.  Closed fracture of right humerus.  Multiple lacerations of hands and lower extremities."  The impact threw the luggage from the trunk into the back of the car and onto the children.  When the police arrived they pulled out Mickey, Jr., and Zoltan. Mickey kept yelling, "My sister, my sister," until the police found little Maria under a pile of suitcases.  Poor, accident-prone Zoltan suffered a concussion and lacerations and managed to come down with mumps while he was in the hospital.  The other children were unharmed.

# *A Formal Feeling* [*]

♥  ♥  ♥

PEOPLE WERE HORRIFIED but not necessarily surprised by
the way Jayne died.  She was almost expected to have that
kind of stark, awful finish.  One publicist thought initially
that the accident was just another stunt that got out of
hand.  Matt feels that Jayne's inability to slow down
doomed her to a violent death.  Marc Britton says she
knew she was going to die young and never felt she had
any time to waste.

In death Jayne was no more serene than she had been in
life.  It was like the partition of Poland: people fought over
her body, her estate and her children just as they had when
she was alive.  The bodies were taken to New Orleans
where the Peerses showed up to claim Jayne.  Mickey arrived, and he and the Peerses went to work to secure the
property found with Jayne, that is, $3740 in cash plus a
diamond ring and bracelet valued at more than $16,000.
Mickey had to leave the next day since he was attending
his daughter's wedding reception in Burbank, California.

* "After Great Pain a Formal Feeling Comes," Emily Dickinson.

○ ○ ○ ○ ○ ○ ○ ○ ○ ○ ○ ○ ○ ○ ○ ○ ○ ○ ○ ○ ○ ○ ○ ○ ○ ○ ○ ○ ○ ○ ○ ○ ○ ○ ○ ○ ○ ○ ○ ○

Tina, eighteen, had married a Vietnam-bound marine in Las Vegas.

Mickey and the Peerses decided that Jayne should be buried in the family plot in Pen Argyl, Pennsylvania. This plan was greeted with disapproval by Cimber, May Mann, Jayne's secretary, Ray Strait, and others who felt that Jayne should be buried in Hollywood, which she had loved.

Ray Strait argued that "Jayne told me many times that she wanted to be buried in Forest Lawn. One day when she was having problems, when she and Mickey were breaking up, she said, 'Ray, let's go for a drive,' and she drove me to the cemetery and we walked.

" 'This has to be the only spot in Hollywood where there aren't any troubles. This is the only place in town where I've found contentment.' "

Mickey argued for the Fairview Cemetery in Pen Argyl. "She loved it out here. Often we would go out to the cemetery to visit the graves of her grandparents and she would say, 'Mickey, someday we will be here too.' And I would say, 'Jaynie, don't be silly. You will never die.' "

As Ross Christena put it, "Level heads prevailed." Jayne was buried at Fairview. It wasn't so much that Mickey had a level head but that the New Orleans court had given him possession of the body. On June 30 the court had found that Jayne's Mexican divorce was not valid, so Mickey was her legal husband.

Mickey's lawyer, Jerome Weber, had flown to New Orleans to make the case that there never was a legal divorce between Jayne and Mickey. Mrs. Peers begged Mickey not to employ Weber. Weber served Mickey well but had to leave the case after some months because he was convicted of taking a bribe while on the Los Angeles district attorney's staff and sent to prison for one to ten.

Mickey and the Peerses had funeral director Gerald Bourgeois transport Jayne to Pennsylvania. It wasn't the

° ° ° ° ° ° ° ° ° ° ° ° ° ° ° ° ° ° ° ° ° ° ° ° ° ° ° ° ° ° ° ° ° ° ° ° ° °

quiet funeral Mickey had longed for. Three thousand policemen came out to handle the crowds. No celebrities
showed up and Mickey was the only former husband
present. As he put it, "We just wanted a little privacy.
Why couldn't the people have left us to weep in peace."
The coffin was covered with a blanket of five hundred roses
with a large heart in the center. At Mickey's suggestion,
the music was "More." Mickey donated an urn with a
gold sash around it, securing thirteen roses and saying,
"Forever and ever, I love you Jayne, Mickey." As he explained, "I always sent her constantly thirteen red roses."

Mickey provided some entertainment by throwing himself on the coffin, kissing it and weeping. Cimber said
that, had he been there, he would have been tempted to
shovel dirt on Mickey. Cimber's lawyer, Bernard Cohen,
explained Cimber's absence. "Mr. Cimber wanted Miss
Mansfield to be buried in the Hollywood style since she
had spent most of her adult life there and loved it. He
said it was his intention to be present for the ceremon-
ies, but he decided his being there would cause controversy." Matt said to the press he didn't go so as not to
cause Vera "pain and anguish." Privately he said he
didn't go because he didn't care.

Ross Christena, faithful to the end, told the press that
Hargitay was "the only man she ever loved." He said,
"Mickey had a big heart-shaped gravestone made at great
expense." And, indeed, there is a huge heart-shaped marble headstone on Jayne's grave.

Back in Hollywood Cimber was busy at work. He set up
private guards all around the pink palace so that Mickey
was refused admission when he returned to the house with
the three children. Weber's statement explained Mickey's
position. "In 1963 Mickey signed an agreement with Jayne
giving her everything. He has no financial interest in the
estate other than the protection of the children's interests is

concerned and wants it to go to all of Jayne's five children equally. I would assume that Cimber would want the same."

Judge Lynch disagreed with the Louisiana decision and appointed Matt official widower and special administrator of the estate on June 30. Matt said, "Although divorce proceedings were pending between Jayne and me there was never an interlocutory decree and I am her husband and next of kin."

Mickey objected to Matt's appointment on July 10 and waived any right to compensation if he were nominated administrator. Mickey, in addition to his claim to being legal widower, objected to Matt on the grounds that he was suing Jayne's estate for $45,000 in back salary which should disqualify him as an interested party.

After two months of litigation with Charles Goldring for the Peerses, plus the Pigues, Matt and Mickey all going at it for administration of the estate, the judge ruled that the estate was to be co-administered by Mickey's and Matt's lawyers. The bulk of the business was to go to Matt's lawyer, Bernard Cohen, who was to get 90 percent of the fees. Matt waived anything in excess of one-sixth of the proceeds of the estate and took $30,000 for dropping his $45,000 suit. He also dropped a $1 million slander suit against Jayne. He was to get all community property acquired during his marriage to Jayne and all proceeds from theater life insurance policies unless payable to the estate. Mickey got off handily with $200,000 from a life insurance policy which Jayne and Goldring, her last business manager, had neglected to make over to Matt. Matt got $20,000 of Mickey's windfall because some of the premiums were paid with community funds from his married days.

Beverly Brody threw herself into the litigation waltz with skill and abandon. Her husband had drawn up a will leaving all his money, some $180,000, to Jayne just eighteen days before he died. "I hereby bequeath and give all my estate, whether personal, real or otherwise, to the only person in the world I love, Jayne Mansfield." Mrs. Brody had the will invalidated on the grounds that Jayne's and Sam's deaths were simultaneous and Jayne's estate couldn't inherit. Mrs. Brody claimed $325,000 from the Mansfield estate in reparation for presents Brody had given Jayne from community funds. Mrs. Brody never got all she asked but she has collected steadily all along. In 1971 she got $7176 from the sale of one of Jayne's sports cars. She got 60 percent of the money Brody had on him when he died and 60 percent of the proceeds from the sale of the jewelry which Jayne was wearing when she died. Mrs. Brody also filed a $1 million negligence suit against Richard Rambo, the driver of the truck which the car struck, as well as the city of New Orleans, which owned the mosquito-spraying machine.

Mrs. Brody had a lot of company in her negligence suit. Matt sued as guardian for Tony, Mickey sued as guardian for Miklos, Zoltan and Maria, and the Pigues sued as Jayne's Marie's guardians. The suits totaled more than $9 million. The settlement was slim. Each child got $22,000 plus $5000 for injuries from Gus Stevens' insurance, an out-of-court settlement. The judge found that Richard Rambo was not a negligent truck driver and that the mosquito sprayer had been a negligent but not a proximate cause of the accident. Ronnie Harrison, however, the driver who had died with Jayne and Sam, was found negligent.

There was trouble back at the palace. Vera and Harry were thrown out by Cimber's guards. They were officially evicted by a judge who ruled that the agreement stated that the house was to be occupied solely by the three children until October 22, when it would be vacated. Vera cried in court and is still very bitter about the decision. Harry

says, "Parents don't count after the child has married."
Vera talks about the distribution of the estate, adding several times that they have had nothing. "Not even an article of clothing." Cimber recalls having thrown them out
because Vera was walking around picking things up saying, "I want this and this. Jaynie promised me that."
Matt told her, "Jaynie died intestate and you're not getting
any of this. It's all for the children." Vera looks at slides
of the palace and gestures dramatically at the pictures, wid-
ening her eyes, lowering her voice, saying, "Where is the
Bentley now? Where is the piano, the portraits? Who has
them?"

Under the court's compromise decision, Cimber was the
surviving spouse and was entitled to receive 50 percent of
the estate. He waived this right and took only one sixth,
splitting equally with the children. Including Mickey's insurance policy the estate was valued at a million dollars.
As time wore on, the attorneys came to feel that the estate
would wind up insolvent because of the expenses incurred
by the administrators and the legal fees which the estate
was paying. It was a lawyers' picnic. They got to collect
executors' fees and handle all the suits which arose from
their executive decisions. For example, Bob Sikking, a
plumber, claimed that Jayne's estate owed him $14,162 for
overhauling the palace pipes. Weber and Cohen said it
was Brody, not Jayne, who called for Sikking and that her
estate was not responsible for the bill. They asked the
court to appoint them to plead the case and to charge their
fees to the estate.

The bills against the estate were of all shapes and sizes.
There were claims from the Venezuelan Hotel Tamanaco,
where Jayne had stayed the previous summer, for $1077.
There was a bill for $7074 for costumes for her act at the
Fremont Hotel. There was a bill for $75 from Bill Knaggs

○ ○ ○ ○ ○ ○ ○ ○ ○ ○ ○ ○ ○ ○ ○ ○ ○ ○ ○ ○ ○ ○ ○ ○ ○ ○ ○ ○ ○ ○ ○ ○ ○ ○ ○ ○ ○ ○ ○ ○

for "make-up for Jayne Mansfield's face for her court date in Santa Monica." Knaggs was turned down.

Mickey, as protector of the children, was suing the estate for a total of $257,532. That was $81,484 for Zoltan, $100,417 for Maria and $75,631 for Mickey, Jr. This suit came under his 1964 divorce settlement in which Jayne agreed to support Mickey, Jr., Zoltan and Maria. Mickey said that he spent $2073 a month to support the children (a far cry from the $71 dollars Jayne Marie cost them in 1958) and that he would have to put additional rooms and baths on his house at 1800 Doheny Drive. Mickey had, meanwhile, remarried. After the funeral he flew to Dallas with the children and the Peerses. He sat in the kitchen with Vera. They were both crying and Vera was holding Mickey's hands, urging him to marry for the sake of the children. Mickey married an airline stewardess. Ellen Hargitay has by all accounts, except perhaps Vera's, been a willing and devoted mother to Jayne's middle three children.

Cimber married Christy Hanak on the second of December 1967. According to him it was a marriage of convenience to provide Tony with a mother. Christy Cimber has legally adopted the little boy and has a son of her own by Matt.

The house and everything in it has been disposed of. The huge pink elephant has been sold twice, and all of its furnishings auctioned off, everything from pianos and coffee tables to hairbrushes and vibrators. Mickey has Jayne's enormous scrapbooks, the ones she paid Jayne Marie to fill. He also has the huge collection of laminated magazine covers which decorated the downstairs at the palace.

After the lawyers had been busy for four years on the estate, they declared that at least $600,000 was going to be used up in fees and expenses and that creditors would be lucky to get thirty-nine cents on the dollar. The history of

Jayne's estate has a Dickensian flavor. People are still suing other people, institutions and cities. The litigation will go on for years, long after Jayne's children are grown up and the estate is gone.

Even in death Jayne still focuses relationships. Matt, for example, is in touch with Jayne Marie. In January 1970, she married a student at the University of Southern California, Barry Lang, whom she had been dating for a couple of years. She was studying at Los Angeles City College. May Mann gave a shower and Matt gave a champagne reception after the Las Vegas ceremony. They have since been divorced. She has plans, she tells Matt, "to get it together in Idaho."

Jayne Marie and Vera stay in touch, although they don't precisely see eye to eye. Vera sent her granddaughter a large, ornate, gold filigree bird which had colored glass eyes and was suspended on a long chain. It cost twenty-five dollars. Jayne Marie wrote back a polite thank-you note explaining that the bird was "not to her taste." Vera suggested that she didn't have to wear it but could frame it "on red velvet and hang it in the house." There was no answer. "I don't understand her," Vera says.

After her death Jayne had a minor musical success. In England Decca brought out a 45 with Jayne singing "As the Clouds Drift By" and "Suey," a ballad, not a hog call. A Decca spokesman rejected the suggestion that the company was capitalizing on her demise. "We are releasing the single — the first we have ever put out by Jayne — because it's a very good record."

Matt says a little wistfully, "She had a half a million in contracts pending when she died." There was a deal in the works to reunite Mickey and Jayne on stage as headliners in a burlesque show. A burlesque house in Jamaica, New York, had also been dickering with Jayne and had offered her $20,000 a week for her act.

Even death didn't protect Jayne. One particularly grue-some instance involves Ross Christena. He booked Jayne in Biloxi. As he said, "She missed three different flights, almost as if someone was telling us something. Delta held a flight, but Jayne was so late they left without her. Finally she flew National."

Christena submitted a claim to the estate in 1968 for $312 — his commission on the Gus Stevens' engagement.